T0009454

# The

# MODERN
# WITCHCRAFT
## Book of
# Tarot

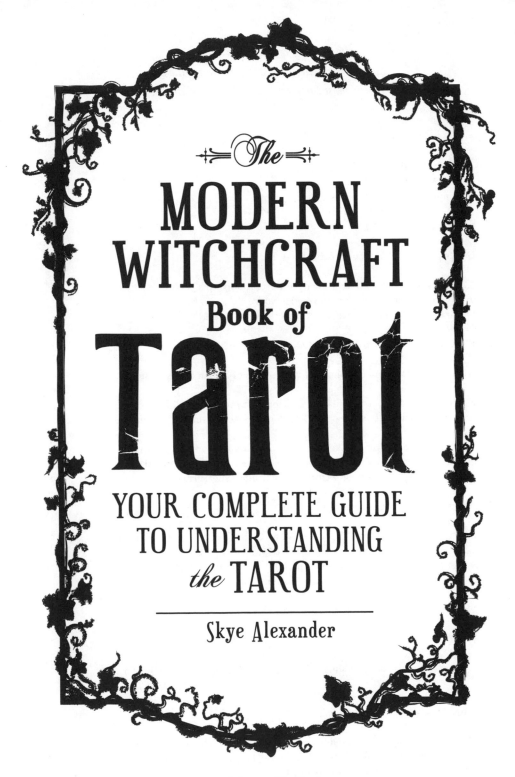

# The
# MODERN
# WITCHCRAFT
## Book of
# Tarot

## YOUR COMPLETE GUIDE
## TO UNDERSTANDING
## *the* TAROT

Skye Alexander

Adams Media
New York  London  Toronto  Sydney  New Delhi

*In memory of Kathleen Valentine,*
*fellow writer, artist, friend, and one of*
*the most talented people I've ever known*

Adams Media
An Imprint of Simon & Schuster, Inc.
100 Technology Center Drive
Stoughton, MA 02072

Copyright © 2017 by Simon & Schuster, Inc.

All rights reserved, including the right to reproduce this book or portions thereof in any form whatsoever. For information address Adams Media Subsidiary Rights Department, 1230 Avenue of the Americas, New York, NY 10020.

First Adams Media hardcover edition MAY 2017

ADAMS MEDIA and colophon are trademarks of Simon and Schuster.

For information about special discounts for bulk purchases, please contact Simon & Schuster Special Sales at 1-866-506-1949 or business@simonandschuster.com.

The Simon & Schuster Speakers Bureau can bring authors to your live event. For more information or to book an event contact the Simon & Schuster Speakers Bureau at 1-866-248-3049 or visit our website at www.simonspeakers.com.

Interior design by Colleen Cunningham

Interior illustrations from the Rider-Waite Tarot Deck® reproduced by permission of U.S. Games Systems, Inc., Stamford, CT 06902 USA. Copyright © 1971 by U.S. Games Systems, Inc. Further reproduction prohibited. The Universal Waite Tarot Deck® is a registered trademark of U.S. Games Systems, Inc.

Manufactured in the United States of America

17 2022

Library of Congress Cataloging-in-Publication Data has been applied for.

ISBN 978-1-5072-0263-0
ISBN 978-1-5072-0264-7 (ebook)

Many of the designations used by manufacturers and sellers to distinguish their products are claimed as trademarks. Where those designations appear in this book and Simon & Schuster, Inc., was aware of a trademark claim, the designations have been printed with initial capital letters.

# *Acknowledgments*

Once again, I wish to express my gratitude to my editors Rebecca Tarr Thomas and Peter Archer, to Stephanie Hannus for her beautiful book design, and to the rest of the Adams Media staff for making this book possible. Best. Team. Ever. I'd also like to thank the Tarot Readers Development and Study Group for many lively discussions, and especially Lara Houston for sharing her insights. Finally, I thank R.L. for inspiring me to begin this journey, which continues to offer new riches every day.

# CONTENTS

# PART II
# INTERPRETING THE CARDS 53

## *Chapter 6:* THE SUIT OF WANDS 55

## *Chapter 7:* THE SUIT OF CUPS 80

## *Chapter 8:* THE SUIT OF PENTACLES 104

*The Modern Witchcraft Book of Tarot*

# Chapter 9: THE SUIT OF SWORDS 129

# Chapter 10: THE MAJOR ARCANA 156

PART III
# READING THE CARDS 207

PART IV
# USING TAROT CARDS IN MAGICK WORK 233

*The Modern Witchcraft Book of Tarot*

# *Introduction*

# RECORDING YOUR MAGICKAL JOURNEY

You probably wouldn't be reading this book if you weren't already curious about the tarot. Many turn to this most elegant oracle because they've reached a crossroads in their lives, or they're in the midst of a crisis and need help. Others are drawn to the tarot initially because of its fascinating artwork. If you're exploring a magickal path as a witch, you've probably stumbled upon the tarot already and want to learn more.

The tarot shows you what lies beneath the surface of situations and what's really going on in those shadowy realms beyond your ordinary range of vision. It lets you gaze into the future and see what's likely to happen. It shines light on murky matters—including your own subconscious motivations. It gives you a broader perspective so you can make better decisions. In short, it's your magick mirror, your wise counselor, a scout who goes ahead to check out the lay of the land, and your brutally honest best friend.

## MAGICK AND THE TAROT

You can't separate the tarot from the practice of magick and witchcraft—they're entwined. Look at the card called The Magician—he's card number one in what's known as the Major Arcana. Right there on the table before him lie the four main tools in a witch's "toolbox": the wand, chalice, pentagram, and sword/athame. Look a little further and you'll realize the four suits of the tarot's Minor Arcana symbolize the four elements (earth, air, fire, and water) that witches and other magicians work with in rituals and spellcraft. For more on all this, consult my books *The Modern Guide to Witchcraft*, *The Modern Witchcraft Spell Book*, and *The Modern Witchcraft Grimoire*.

The images that illustrate this book were created by two noted magick workers, Arthur Edward Waite and Pamela Colman Smith, both members of an influential mystical order known as the Hermetic Order of the Golden Dawn. Consequently, the symbols, colors, numbers, and other features on the cards convey magickal information. Although many people start their exploration into the tarot with this popular pack of cards, you can use any deck that appeals to you—and there are thousands from which to choose. Many decks also incorporate astrology, the Kabbalah, shamanism, and other magickal systems familiar to witches.

---

### Choose the Right Deck

Choosing a tarot deck is a highly personal matter. You'll find a number of decks designed with witches in mind, including the Witches Tarot, Tarot of the Witches, Everyday Witch Tarot, and Green Witch Tarot. You might also like the Sacred Circle Tarot and the Faery Wicca Tarot.

---

# THE TAROT'S HISTORY AND MYSTERY

The tarot's roots go back at least to the fifteenth century, and perhaps a lot farther. Many researchers believe it started out as a card game in Renaissance Europe, although other theories abound. In Chapter 2, you can read about some of the ways people in those days used cards both for entertainment and for telling fortunes. The tarot's history is rich, complex, and a bit murky. It will probably always remain a mystery—and that's part of its appeal.

If you want to learn more about the tarot's origins and evolution, you'll find lots of interesting material online and in the many books that have been written about this enigmatic oracle, in addition to what I touch on here. If you don't care, you can skip right over that chapter.

You don't need to know anything about where the tarot came from or how it evolved in order to use it. The whole point of this book is to jump right in. Still, you might enjoy discovering the who, what, when, where, and why behind this amazing oracle that's held us in its thrall all these centuries.

## HOW TO USE THIS BOOK

Getting a tarot reading from a professional cartomancer can be a most educational and enlightening experience. However, you can do readings for yourself—in fact, many people learn the meanings of the cards by experimenting on themselves. It isn't necessary for every practicing witch to be able to do tarot readings, but it's a very useful skill that will help you in other aspects of your craft.

In writing this book, I've tried to make an esoteric and intricate mystical system accessible to those of you who are just starting out on this journey. To that end, I've explained in Part II each of the seventy-eight cards of a typical tarot deck in what I hope is a user-friendly way, combining commonly accepted interpretations with what I've gleaned from my many years of experience. Until you become proficient at doing readings, you can look up these general meanings. With practice, you'll become adept at interpretation and come to your own, unique understanding of the tarot.

In Part III, I've included some of my favorite tarot "spreads"—patterns that put the individual cards into a context during a reading. In Part IV, I share lots of spells from my personal grimoire that use tarot cards in magickal ways.

In time, you may decide to purchase more than one tarot pack. I recommend using one for readings and another for magick work. If you decide to do readings for other people, I suggest using one deck for yourself and another when you read for other people. That means you may eventually become the proud owner of at least three tarot packs. Over the years, I've owned about 200 different decks—yes, they can get addicting. Many people collect tarot packs for the artwork alone, and some rare, famous decks now reside in museums or the private collections of wealthy individuals.

# DOES THE TAROT WORK?

Regardless of the beauty, wonder, and mystery of the tarot, it probably wouldn't have stood the test of time if it didn't work—as an oracle, a tool for self-discovery, a meditation aid, a guide for personal growth, and an adjunct to magickal practice. Although our ancestors may have dabbled in it as a mere amusement, that's not why most of us turn to the tarot today.

Perhaps you're still asking: Can the tarot really predict the future and reveal hidden information? Can it give me insight into the past and how I might handle the present? Can it help me solve problems in my life, improve my relationships with others, and fulfill my potential?

The best way to find out is to try it yourself.

# PART I

# Getting *to* Know *the* Tarot

# Chapter 1

# A LITTLE BIT ABOUT ORACLES

What will tomorrow bring? Since ancient times, people throughout the world have sought answers to this question by consulting oracles. As a witch, you may already be familiar with oracles and even use them yourself. Do you gaze into a treasured crystal ball or a magick mirror to see beyond your ordinary realm of vision? Watch smoke waft away from a ritual fire or stare into the flickering flame of a candle to gain insight? Have you cast runes, consulted the *I Ching*, or dowsed with a pendulum in search of answers? Or perhaps asked a psychic or shaman for advice?

The most famous oracle of all in the ancient world was the Oracle at Delphi. Thousands of years ago, the Greeks trekked to Mount Parnassus (about 75 miles from Athens) to petition this famous priestess for advice. While in a trance, she tuned in to the divine realm and allowed a deity to speak through her. Meanwhile in China, court astrologers of the Zhou dynasty interpreted upcoming events in the stars, clouds, rain, and wind. The rulers of ancient Sumeria and Babylonia looked to diviner priests to reveal the future. In today's confusing world, we can still turn to oracles for insight and guidance—sometimes oracles are the only reliable road maps.

# WHAT IS AN ORACLE ANYWAY?

Divination is the art of predicting the future. The word literally means "the practice of letting the divine realm manifest." An oracle may be a person with special abilities to see beyond the limits of the visible world. Physical tools such as tarot cards and runes are also called oracles.

Oracles give you access to information you can't perceive through ordinary means. They connect you with your subconscious or inner knowing. They also serve as a link to divine wisdom or higher mind. When you ask an oracle for advice, some part of you may already know the answer to your question—the oracle enables you to access that knowledge hidden deep within and bring it into the open so you can use it. Through the use of oracles you can even tap into cosmic knowledge contained in what's sometimes called the Akashic Record.

> *"The whole world is an omen and a sign. Why look so wistfully in a corner?... The voice of divination resounds everywhere and runs to waste unheard, unregarded, as the mountains echo with the bleatings of cattle."*
>
> —RALPH WALDO EMERSON

## Everyday Oracles

You've already used oracles, even if you didn't know it. Every time you toss a coin and call "heads" or "tails" before making a decision, you're consulting an oracle. When you look at a woolly caterpillar's coloring to determine whether the coming winter will be harsh or mild, you're divining the future. Remember those daisy petals you plucked when you were a kid to find out if the person you had a crush on loved you? That flower was an oracle too.

Predictive signs exist around you all the time, everywhere, if you choose to see them. When I find coins on the ground, for instance, I know I'll soon receive money. Many of us see visions or images in dreams that foretell upcoming situations. Some people randomly open a favorite book or religious text and consider the first passage they read as guidance. Others turn on the radio and listen for meaning in the first song that plays. The appearance of certain animals and birds may also hold significance. Anything can be an oracle. The tarot, in my opinion, is one of the most elegant and intricate of all—which is why it's remained so popular all these years.

---

### Frithirs

Celtic oracles known as *frithirs* served as prognosticators for the Scots. Four times a year, on the first Monday of each quarter, the frithir would fast, then step outside blindfolded just before sunrise. Upon removing her blindfold, she opened her eyes and interpreted the meaning of the first thing she saw.

---

## Using Oracles

Oracles operate on the principle that symbols trigger intuition. (We'll talk more about symbols in Chapter 3.) When you lay out tarot cards, cast runes, or scry with a crystal ball, you open yourself to receive information from your higher mind and the spirit world. As witches, we continually seek guidance and input from the higher realms, as well as from our own inner wisdom. We hone our intuition through meditation, dreamwork, ritual, spellcasting, and other practices. We know we're integrally connected with our own beautiful planet and with the cosmos. We realize we can benefit—and help others—if we establish better connections between our conscious awareness and those other wondrous, mysterious loci of wisdom that exist within and around us. That's why we turn to oracles, because they serve as conduits between heaven and earth and let us see situations from a broader perspective.

Your willingness to receive guidance from a source other than your everyday, rational thinking will enable you to gain clear, meaningful insights from the tarot and other oracles. If you're skeptical about the possibility of seeing into the future or doubt the validity of the answers you receive, you'll block the flow of information. Try to keep an open mind. You have everything to gain and nothing to lose.

# POPULAR ORACLES

Lots of divination devices and systems can help you gain insight into your past, present, and future. You may already be familiar with some of them—or at least you're curious about them. Some are complex and require time to master. Astrology and tarot fall into this category, but don't let that deter you from studying either—the benefits will be worth the effort. Others, such as the Ouija board, can be used successfully by novices. Anything can serve as an oracle.

---

### Divining from Seashells

In *Ocean Oracle*, Michelle "Shelley" Hanson considers 200 seashells as tools for divination. According to Hanson, "When you are attracted to—or bothered by—a particular shell, messages can surface from the wisdom attached to that shell. Similar to a tarot reading, the shells can reveal valuable information and facilitate positive growth."

---

## Divination Devices

Beautifully illustrated tarot cards are the most popular oracle—you can choose from literally thousands of decks on the market. In addition to the tarot, you might like to try some of the following popular divination devices. These tools let you discover more about yourself and give you a glimpse of what's likely to happen in the future. They can also alert you to aspects of situations you might not be aware of or reveal things about people—and yourself—that you didn't realize before.

- Runes—The word *rune* means "secret" or "mystery." Most people think of the early Norse alphabet when they hear the word *runes*. (If you're a fan of J.R.R. Tolkien's books, you've already heard about runes and perhaps used them.) The most popular alphabet contains twenty-four letters, and each letter is named for an animal, object, condition, or deity. If you have Celtic blood running in your veins, you might enjoy consulting Ogham runes, based on trees.
- Pendulum—A pendulum usually consists of a small weight, such as a crystal, hung from a short chain or cord. You hold the chain, letting the pendulum "bob" dangle at the end of it, while you ask a simple question. The pendulum's movement—back and forth, side to side, around and around—has meaning and answers your question.
- *I Ching*—For three thousand years, the *I Ching* (pronounced ee-ching), or *Book of Changes*, has been used in China and the East.

*The Modern Witchcraft Book of Tarot*

This ancient oracle, which deals with the relationships between individuals, society, and the Divine, is thought to have been created by Confucius. It contains sixty-four patterns called hexagrams, each made up of six lines. Each hexagram and each line within it has a meaning.

- Crystals—When you think of a fortuneteller, does the image of a woman in a turban gazing into a crystal ball come to mind? You really can look into a crystal and see beyond your normal range of vision. A genuine crystal ball or large piece of quartz crystal contains all sorts of natural irregularities that help spark your imagination. Turn it in different directions and you'll see different scenarios. This is called scrying. You can also scry with other reflective surfaces, such as dark mirrors or pools of water.

---

### Nostradamus's Scrying

The famous sixteenth-century seer Nostradamus gazed into a bowl of water for hours at a time, watching visions of the future appear before him. Scrying in this manner enabled him to predict events that would occur centuries later.

---

## Divination Systems

The tarot is both a device and a system for gaining insight, guidance, and answers to life's questions. In the chapters that follow, we'll delve into the secrets of this magickal oracle. As you pursue your path of wisdom, you might also enjoy learning more about other predictive systems that witches have studied and turned to since ancient times, including:

- Astrology—You probably know your sun sign, but that's just the tip of the iceberg. If you consult with a professional astrologer, he or she will calculate a birth chart for you that shows the positions of not only the sun at the moment of your birth but also the moon and planets (and other things too), as well as their relationships to each other and to the earth. Each heavenly body has its own energies that impact human beings, social and political situations, weather patterns, and earth changes. As you work with the tarot, you'll discover many connections between it and astrology. The four suits of the tarot's Minor Arcana, for instance, correspond to the four elements fundamental to astrology: earth, air, fire, and water.

*"The four elements . . . are the basic building blocks of all material structures and organic wholes. Each element represents a basic kind of energy and consciousness that operates within each of us."*

—STEPHEN ARROYO, *ASTROLOGY, PSYCHOLOGY,*

*AND THE FOUR ELEMENTS*

- Numerology—Why are some years filled with activity and adventure, whereas others seem uneventful or calm? The answer lies in the predictive side of numerology. Each number has a distinctive resonance that corresponds to certain situations, feelings, or actions. One, for example, is the number of beginnings; five the number of change. By examining the numbers in a date, you can get a good idea of what might happen then. (We'll talk about number symbolism in Chapter 4. My book *The Everything® Wicca and Witchcraft Book* discusses other aspects of numerology and explains how to use it.) Numerology is an integral part of the tarot, as you'll soon see. The numbers on the cards hold secret meanings, and we'll talk about those in later chapters of this book.

The twenty-first century confronts us with unprecedented opportunities and challenges, many of which have no easy answers. The tarot and other divination aids serve as beacons, shining light into the darkness to help us see where we're going. Once you learn the symbolic language of the cards, you'll be able to access the hidden wisdom of the tarot and the magick behind it. In Part IV of this book, you'll even discover ways to use the cards in spellwork.

Explore. Engage your curiosity. Use your imagination. Keep an open mind and an open heart. Your future really is in the cards!

## Chapter 2

# THE ORIGINS OF THE TAROT

For hundreds of years, people like you have turned to this beautiful oracle for advice, guidance, and answers to important questions. Many theories exist about the tarot's beginnings. One says the cards date back more than 2,000 years to ancient Egypt and the great library in Alexandria. Another story tells us the Crusaders brought the tarot back with them from the Middle East. Yet another credits the Romani people with introducing the cards into Europe.

> *"R.J. Stewart suggests that the tarot had its origins in 'the storytelling traditions and images preserved by travelling entertainers, originally the bards or* filid *of Celtic culture.' He points out that the images of the tarot have clear connections with images described in the* Vita Merlini, *a text that pre-dates the earliest known tarot deck by three centuries. It clearly describes The Empress, The Hanged Man, the Wheel of Fortune, The Fool, and so on, which are derived from the bardic Celtic tradition of preserving images of the gods, goddesses, and cosmology."*
> —ANNA FRANKLIN, THE SACRED CIRCLE TAROT

## RENAISSANCE CARDS GAMES OF THE RICH AND FAMOUS

We may never know if these theories hold truth. However, we do know there's a link between the tarot and Renaissance playing cards. You can see similarities in our modern-day poker decks as well.

## Italy's Tarocchi

Beginning in the 1400s, Italian aristocrats used cards called *trionfi* (triumphs) to play a game known as *Il Trionfos*.

Wealthy people commissioned artists to create the cards, which were hand-painted or printed with carved woodblocks. These weren't mere gambling games, though—they were exercises in creativity. Players took the themes shown on the cards and used them as springboards for composing poems about each other. The earliest deck that still exists today is also one of the most beautiful: the Visconti Tarot, commissioned by the Duke of Milan in the mid-1400s. Many of the original cards from this deck, painted on gold and silver foil, are now housed in New York's Morgan Library & Museum.

## Islamic Card Games

Playing card games became popular in the Arab world too, in the fourteenth and fifteenth centuries—especially among the wealthy classes and high-ranking members of the military. One handsome deck, known as the Mamluk pack, had an important influence on the tarot as we know it. This deck contained four suits—coins, cups, swords, and polo sticks—as well as ten numbered cards and four court cards per suit, similar to what we see in the Minor Arcana today. We can assume the cards were used for telling fortunes as well as for gaming because they feature prognosticating rhymes such as:

*As for the present that rejoices, thy heart will soon open up.*

*O thou who hast possessions, remain happy and thou shalt have a pleasant life.*

*With the sword of happiness I shall redeem a beloved who will afterwards take my life.*

What remains of the original deck now resides in Istanbul's Topkapi Museum, but you can see pictures of it on the website the World of Playing Cards at www.wopc.co.uk.

## The Spanish Card Game of Love

The Spanish nobility in the fifteenth century played a game called *Juego de Naypes* with forty-nine colorful cards. These cards were used to tell fortunes and reveal secrets, particularly in matters of love. Divided into four suits based on women—maidens, wives, widows, and nuns—the cards showed what someone loved or desired most. Each card had a verse written on it, composed of the same number of lines as the card's number.

By the seventeenth century, professional "cartomancers" (fortune-tellers who saw the future in the cards) were plying their trade in Spain. These card readers laid out cards in patterns much like the tarot spreads we use today.

> "[In the nineteenth century] a French occultist who called himself Eliphas Lévi linked the cards to the large and complex body of Jewish mysticism and theosophy known as Kabbalah. The historic basis for such a connection is questionable; the thousands of pages of Kabbalistic texts make no mention of cards or paintings. And yet, the idea remains compelling. The Kabbalah structures itself around the twenty-two letters of the Hebrew alphabet; the Major Arcana consists of twenty-two trumps. The Kabbalah speaks of four worlds of existence and ten stations on the tree of life; the Tarot contains four suits, each with ten numbered cards and four court cards."
>
> —RACHEL POLLACK, SALVADOR DALI'S TAROT

# TAROT IN THE MODERN ERA

Many early tarot decks featured beautiful designs but lacked the storytelling imagery we're familiar with today. This made them more challenging to read. Along with an interest in Spiritualism and ritual magick at the turn of the twentieth century came a renewed enthusiasm for the tarot—and a new way of relating to it.

### The Tarot's Two Books

The tarot decks we use today are made up of two "books": the Major Arcana and the Minor Arcana. The word *arcana* means "mysteries or secrets." The Minor Arcana in a typical deck contains fifty-six cards: four suits with ten numbered cards and four court cards in each. It resembles the early playing cards from the Renaissance as well as our present-day poker decks (except, of course, poker decks contain only three court cards per suit). The Major Arcana consists of twenty-two cards, which also bear numbers from zero (The Fool) to twenty-one (The World).

The Minor Arcana cards describe mundane, everyday events and experiences. Those in the Major Arcana show cosmic, spiritual, or divine forces—destiny or fate, if you like—at work.

> *"The Major Arcana cards deal directly with facets of our soul: the light, the dark, our dreams, fears, wishes, and determinations."*
> —JANE STERN, *CONFESSIONS OF A TAROT READER*

### The Rider-Waite-Smith Deck

In 1909, the tarot underwent a significant change in its long and colorful history. Arthur Edward Waite, one of the most noted occultists of the modern era, commissioned Pamela Colman Smith, an artist and theatrical designer, to create a unique tarot deck. Both individuals were members of the Hermetic Order of the Golden Dawn, an influential mystical society of which Waite became the Grand Master—that's why the cards in this pack contain magickal symbols associated with the Golden Dawn. Under Waite's guidance, Smith produced seventy-eight paintings, which became the cards of the tarot deck. The London company, William Rider & Son, published the deck in 1910.

The most notable feature of this deck was that all the cards, not only the Major Arcana, depicted "storytelling" scenes that conveyed their meanings. Now you could look at a card and get a sense of what it was all about. The pictures let you read the cards intuitively. Glance at the Ten of Swords, which shows a man lying on the ground with ten swords sticking in his back, and you immediately think of treachery, deception, and pain. The joyful young women dancing on the Three of Cups clearly speak of revelry, happy times, and friendship.

Since the deck's initial publication, a number of variations have evolved. Many other tarot decks have also been based on Smith's simple yet powerful designs. More than a hundred years after its creation, the Rider-Waite-Smith tarot remains the most popular and influential deck today.

### The Thoth Tarot

People tend to love or hate the Thoth Tarot, another of the most important decks of the twentieth century. Painted by Lady Frieda Harris under the direction of the infamous English occultist and "bad boy" magician, Aleister Crowley, between 1938 and 1943, its striking images and brilliant colors appeal to some tarotists and disturb others—which isn't surprising considering the controversial man behind the deck's creation. It wasn't published until 1969, however, after both Crowley and Harris had died, and has never been out of print since.

The Thoth Tarot's imagery draws on many different esoteric, scientific, spiritual, and philosophical systems including alchemy, astrology, and magick. (Thoth, by the way, was an important deity and scribe to the gods in Egyptian mythology.) The names Crowley gave to the Major Arcana cards in his pack differ somewhat from those in the Rider-Waite-Smith deck—for example, he called card number fourteen Art instead of Temperance. Crowley also chose different names for some of the court cards, which readers may find confusing.

> *"The Tarot is a pictorial representation of the Forces of Nature as conceived by the Ancients according to a conventional symbolism. At first sight one would suppose this arrangement to be arbitrary, but it is not. It is necessitated by the structure of the universe, and in particular of the Solar System, as symbolized by the Holy Qabalah."*
> —ALEISTER CROWLEY, THE BOOK OF THOTH

### Tarot Innovations

Today, tens of thousands of tarot decks exist, and artists are designing more all the time. Whether you're of Celtic, Japanese, or Native American heritage, enjoy gardening or baseball, have a fondness for cats or unicorns, you'll find a deck that speaks to you. Vampires, zombies, and even gummy bears have found their way into the tarot.

Nearly all tarot cards are rectangular, although one notable deck—the Motherpeace Tarot—features round cards. It hit the marketplace in the 1970s along with the rise of feminism, and celebrates 30,000 years of women's culture. Some decks have oversized cards, such as those in the Renaissance packs; others are made up of miniature cards that fit easily into your pocket or purse. Some contain more than the usual seventy-eight cards, perhaps even a few blank ones so you can create your own. Some tarot decks come packaged with companion books that interpret the cards according to their designers' philosophy or focus.

Many original decks that have not been printed can be viewed online. Blog sites and Facebook groups provide lively forums for tarot enthusiasts to share ideas. You can even get free, instant tarot readings online. As technology continues developing, we'll undoubtedly see more exciting innovations, for the tarot continues to be a living, evolving medium.

## MAGICK, WITCHCRAFT, AND THE TAROT

Maybe you've been walking the path of the witch for years and have recently developed an interest in the tarot. Or, after reading tarot cards for a while, you've found your way—perhaps by following the oracle's guidance—into the witches' world. However you got here, whatever inspired you to tread this path, welcome!

> *"Witches have had a special relationship with the tarot cards for centuries. Their lives have always been steeped in magic and mystery. Witches are natural clairvoyants and ideal psychic readers because they do not separate the spiritual from the mundane in their daily lives . . . Witches know that it is not enough to simply be psychic and see the future. We have a magical responsibility to share the power with our clients, helping them to avoid problems and reach life's fullest potential."*
>
> —WWW.SALEMTAROT.COM

Not all witches work with the tarot, but many do. As mentioned in the introduction, the tarot and witchcraft have many connections. When you look at The Magician, you'll instantly recognize on the card four tools witches use in magick work: the wand, chalice, pentagram, and sword/athame. The magus depicted here raises one hand toward the sky and points the other at the ground, representing the axiom "as above, so below" and the union of heaven and earth. In some decks, these four tools also appear on the card called The World. The four suits of the Minor Arcana are named for these tools and symbolize the four elements—fire, water, earth, and air respectively—that witches recognize as the energetic forces operating in our world.

*The Modern Witchcraft Book of Tarot*

## Elements, Directions, and Angels

Witches also associate the four elements with the four directions and the four archangels:

- Raphael, angel of air, guards the east.
- Michael, angel of fire, watches over the south.
- Gabriel, angel of water, presides over the west.
- Uriel, angel of earth, governs the north.

When you cast a circle for a ritual or other magick work, you may call upon the archangels of air, fire, water, and earth to assist you and evoke the powers of the elements. Take a look at The World card in the Rider-Waite-Smith deck—you'll notice winged symbols of the elements in the corners of the card, representing the archangels and the forces of the universe.

In the next chapter, we'll examine the symbols on tarot cards in greater depth. As Joseph Campbell wrote in *The Hero with a Thousand Faces*, "It has always been the prime function of mythology and rite to supply the symbols that carry the human spirit forward." The same might be said of the tarot.

# Chapter 3

# THE LANGUAGE OF SYMBOLS

Pick a card from your tarot deck. You'll see all sorts of images on it—some you'll recognize, some you may not. Regardless of whether you understand consciously what these pictures mean, your subconscious reacts to them. Like dream imagery, symbols speak to us at a deep level and trigger insights in an immediate, powerful way. Remember the old saying, "A picture's worth a thousand words"? When you're working with the tarot, that's certainly true.

Symbols and pictures offer other advantages over words too. They bypass the analytical, orderly left brain and strike up a lively conversation with the imaginative, intuitive right brain. They inspire you to think but don't tell you what to think.

*"Tarot is above all a symbolic system of self-knowledge, self-integration, and self-transformation. Vital to integration is the union of opposites within, a process which Jung says 'on a higher level of consciousness is not a rational thing, nor is it a matter of will; it is a psychic process of development which expresses itself in symbols.'"*
—RICHARD ROBERTS, *THE ORIGINAL TAROT & YOU*

# COLOR SYMBOLISM

Even before you get to the specific symbols, you'll probably notice the colors on the card. Many tarot decks display vivid and beautiful color palettes. These colors aren't purely decorative—they contain symbolic, spiritual, psychological, and physiological properties as well. Tarot artists, like other artists, use colors to convey moods and messages to those who view them.

## Colors and the Elements

In the practice of magick, colors correspond to the four elements: fire, water, earth, and air. We can experience these elements in the natural world, but they have spiritual and symbolic properties as well. Understanding these properties and their color correspondences can help you interpret the cards and their magickal meanings.

In both the tarot and in Western magick (remember, the tarot and magick are integrally linked), red is associated with the fire element, blue with water, green with earth, and yellow with air. Additionally, each of the tarot's four suits relates to one of these elements. (We'll talk more about these suits soon.) Many tarot readers link wands with fire, cups with water, pentacles with earth, and swords with air. As a result, tarot artists may, for example, emphasize red on cards in the suit of wands and blue on the cups cards to trigger subconscious responses and insights. Not everyone or every deck follows this order, though.

---

### Colors and the Four Directions

When casting a circle for a spell or ritual, you may have called upon the energies of the four directions and the beings who guard the quarters. Witches associate a color with each of these directions: yellow with east, red with south, blue with west, and green with north. You may want to place a candle or other object of the appropriate color at each of the directions in your home or outdoors—wherever you do magickal workings.

---

## Hidden Meanings in Colors

Color symbolism involves more than the four suits of the Minor Arcana. Each color you see has special meanings that resonate with us intuitively. In some cases, colors hold cultural or personal significances that may vary according to an individual's traditions, nationality, or belief system. Many, however, hold universal symbolism.

## Colors and Cultures

Colors have different connections and symbolism in different cultures. For instance, Chinese brides wear red, a color of good fortune in that culture. In China, white is considered a color of mourning. For witches, black denotes power, not grief. Individuals also respond in unique ways to certain colors. For instance, you may be drawn to colors that correspond to your zodiac sign. I have a Taurus friend who always wears earth tones; I'm an Aquarian and I love sky blue and cobalt.

Look at several tarot packs and notice how the artists who designed them used colors to express certain qualities. The following table lists qualities generally associated with the different hues:

| Color | Qualities |
|---|---|
| red | passion, vitality, courage |
| orange | warmth, energy, activity, drive, confidence |
| yellow | creativity, optimism, enthusiasm |
| green | healing, growth, fertility, prosperity |
| light blue | purity, serenity, mental clarity, compassion |
| royal blue | loyalty, insight, inspiration, independence |
| indigo | intuition, focus, stability |
| purple | wisdom, spirituality, power |
| white | purity, wholeness, protection |
| black | power, the unconscious, banishing, wisdom |
| pink | love, friendship, affection, joy, self-esteem |
| brown | grounding, permanence, practicality |

# THE SUITS OF THE MINOR ARCANA

Regardless of what "spin" a particular artist puts on his or her deck, certain basic concepts will most likely prevail. The four suits in what's known as the Minor Arcana are fundamental to the tarot's structure and composition. As mentioned earlier, these suits correspond to the four elements: fire, water, earth, and air.

As we discussed in Chapter 2, tarot cards and ordinary playing cards have a close association—they may have evolved from the same source. Therefore, it's no surprise that a poker deck is also divided into four suits and that these suits correspond to the ones in the tarot: clubs/wands, hearts/cups, diamonds/pentacles, and spades/swords.

---

### Different Interpretations

Not everyone agrees with the connections I make between the suits of the tarot and those in a poker deck. For example, A.E. Waite, the occultist who inspired the Rider-Waite-Smith tarot, connected wands with diamonds, swords with clubs, and pentacles with spades. Use your own judgment and intuition as you work with the cards—you may not even feel a need to link playing cards with the tarot.

---

The suits also symbolize the feminine and masculine forces operating in our universe. You can easily spot the phallic symbolism in the suits of wands and swords—and indeed, witches associate the elements fire and air, with which these suits are linked, with masculine or yang energy. Cups bring to mind the shape of the womb, and the suit's link with the water element clearly connects cups with the feminine principle. The pentacle—or pentagram—symbolizes the human body; its five points represent the head, arms, and legs.

## *Wands*

The suit of wands (also called rods, staves, clubs, batons, and other terms) corresponds to the element of fire. Fire is active, outer-directed, and linked with will, self-expression, and inspiration. It suggests expansion and personal power. Wands often describe career-related issues, so you may see them turning up in questions regarding your job, a creative endeavor, or an avocation about which you feel passionate.

You may be familiar with the wands Harry Potter and his friends use, which resemble an orchestra conductor's baton. However, the wands depicted on tarot cards aren't so wimpy. In the Rider-Waite-Smith deck, for example, wands appear as wooden staffs taller than a man and sprouting leaves.

Figures on the wands cards (in storytelling decks) are frequently shown as warriors, heroes, or leaders—dynamic and inspired people who charge forth into life with confidence and enthusiasm. They may ride proud steeds, wave flags, or wear garlands. Whatever they're doing, they appear to be enjoying themselves. Even when they face challenges, these courageous and hardy individuals seem capable of handling the difficulties placed before them and succeeding at whatever they undertake.

When wands appear in a reading, it's usually an indication that some sort of action or growth is afoot. You might be embarking on an adventure of some kind or may be required to muster your courage in a challenging endeavor. Wands may also prod you to have fun, take some risks, assert yourself, or be creative.

*"Wand Power Teach Me to Merge Ego with Sacred Self."*
—KISMA K. STEPANICH, *FAERY WICCA TAROT*

## Cups

The suit of cups (also called chalices or vessels) is associated with the element of water. Water's energy is receptive, inner-directed, reflective, and connected with the emotions, creativity, and intuition. In the tarot, cups are usually shown as chalices or goblets, but some decks picture them as bowls, cauldrons, vases, urns, pitchers, coffee mugs, beer steins, or bottles. Regardless of the imagery, the principle is the same—cups signify the ability to receive and hold.

Because the suit of cups represents the emotions, the people on the cards are frequently shown in relationships of some kind: romantic, familial, or friendly. A reading that contains many cups emphasizes emotions and/or relationships. The individual cards and how they turn up in a reading will reveal whether these interactions are pleasurable or painful.

## Pentacles

Pentacles or pentagrams correspond to the earth element. Like water, earth is a feminine/yin energy that relates to our planet as the source of sustenance, security, and stability. Some tarot decks portray the suit as coins or discs, or even as shields, stones, shells, crystals, wheels, or loaves of bread. Regardless of the actual image used, the suit symbolizes physical resources, the body, values, practical concerns, material goods, property, and forms of monetary exchange—things that sustain us on the earthly plane.

### Witches' Pentagrams

The pentagram witches favor features a five-pointed star with a circle around it. The circle encloses the energy of the star (which represents the physical body) and provides protection. In Texas, where I live, people display pentagrams everywhere—on their homes, municipal buildings, parks, and city squares—although most don't make the connection. Texas Rangers wore the "Lone Star" badges, and these pentagrams may have saved some lives.

Storytelling decks often depict people on the pentacles cards engaged in some form of work or commerce. On some cards, these people enjoy the fruits of their labors and the things money can buy; on others they suffer in poverty. When pentacles appear in a spread, it's usually a sign that financial or material matters are prominent in the mind of the person for whom the reading is being done. In some cases, these cards may signify physical or health issues, or other situations involving the body. Depending on the cards, this suit may suggest a need to focus on practical concerns or, conversely, that one is putting too much emphasis on material things.

*"Relationships are the Holy Spirit's laboratories in which He brings together people who have the maximal opportunity for mutual growth. He appraises who can learn most from whom at any given time, and then assigns them to each other."*
—MARIANNE WILLIAMSON, *A RETURN TO LOVE*

### The Pentagram in Eden

If you cut an apple in half, you'll see its seeds form a five-pointed star. Thus, the story of the Garden of Eden, when Eve gives Adam the apple to eat, describes the soul's descent into the physical body.

## Swords

The suit of swords relates to the element of air. Although usually depicted as a mighty battle sword, some decks illustrate the suit as ordinary knives, athames (ritual daggers used by witches and other magick workers), scythes, axes, or spears. Regardless of how it's represented, the cutting "weapon" is the intellect. As such, swords symbolize rational thinking, logic, analysis, communication, and the power of the mind.

### Excalibur

The most famous of all swords, of course, is King Arthur's Excalibur. In the "Sword in the Stone" legend, the sword is lodged in a stone and can be withdrawn only by the rightful king: Arthur. In a later legend, popularized by Sir Thomas Malory, Arthur receives the sword from the Lady of the Lake. Interestingly, in both tales the powerful masculine weapon is kept safe for Arthur by a feminine source: earth or water.

Storytelling decks frequently show the characters on the swords cards as warriors, scholars, sages, teachers, or seekers—serious individuals who pursue the answers to life's great questions. Often the images reveal suffering or strife, perhaps indicating the struggle involved in transforming experience into knowledge. As such, they illustrate Rudolf Steiner's statement, "Wisdom is crystallized pain."

When swords turn up in a reading, it usually means that mental or verbal activity is a priority. Perhaps you're thinking too much, worrying and over-analyzing a situation. Or, you might need to use your head to examine an issue clearly and rationally. Communication may benefit you now, or you may need to use logic and discrimination to cut through a murky situation.

*The Modern Witchcraft Book of Tarot*

*"Working with the magic of tarot symbolism brings us to the heart center, above the mundane realities of the first three chakras. On a higher metaphysical level, working with tarot cards can open up the seventh chakra of divine inspiration and the sixth chakra of creative vision. Insight communicated through the fifth chakra, tempered with compassion of the fourth chakra, can create a tarot interpretation of the most effective healing alchemy."*

—SUSAN LEVITT, *INTRODUCTION TO TAROT*

## POPULAR SYMBOLS

Symbols embody the essence of whatever they stand for—they aren't merely a convenient form of shorthand. That's why they have such power, why they appear in diverse and widely separated cultures, and why they have endured for millennia.

Tarot artists intentionally choose symbols from various spiritual, cultural, magickal, and psychological traditions to convey information directly to your subconscious. Like myths, symbols transcend the boundaries of religion, nationality, and time, presenting universal themes and concepts that people everywhere can relate to. The following table shows a number of common, universally understood symbols that often appear on tarot cards, along with their usual meanings.

*"When the soul wishes to experience something, she throws an image of the experience out before her and enters into her own image."*

—MEISTER ECKHART

| Symbol | Meaning |
|---|---|
| Circle | Wholeness, unity, protection, continuity |
| Square | Stability, equality, structure |
| Triangle | Trinity, three-dimensional existence, movement |
| Downward triangle | Divine feminine, earth or water elements |
| Upward triangle | Divine masculine, fire or air elements |
| Star | Hope, promise |

| Symbol | Meaning |
|---|---|
| Five-pointed star | Protection, the human body, physical incarnation |
| Six-pointed star | Union of male/female or earth/sky, integration, manifestation |
| Vertical line | Movement, heaven, sky, masculine energy |
| Horizontal line | Stability, earth, feminine energy |
| Cross | Union of male/female or earth/sky, integration, manifestation |
| Spiral | Life energy, renewal, movement toward the center |
| Sun | Clarity, vitality, optimism, contentment, masculine energy |
| Moon | Secrets, intuition, emotions, feminine energy |
| Dove | Peace, reconciliation, promise |
| Crane | Wisdom |
| Rose | Love |
| Mountain | Challenge, vision, achievement |
| Water | Emotions, the unknown depths of the psyche |
| Snake | Transformation, hidden knowledge, kundalini energy |
| Egg | Birth, fertility |
| Rainbow | Renewal, hope, happiness |
| Book | Knowledge |
| Lantern | Guidance, clarity, hope |
| Bridge | Connection, harmony, overcoming difficulty |
| Tree | Knowledge, growth, protection, strength |
| Butterfly | Transformation |

Of course, we all have our own personal symbols as well, which mean something special to us although other people may not relate to them in the same way. When studying the symbolism in the tarot, remember that your own responses and interpretations are what count most. Cars

*The Modern Witchcraft Book of Tarot*

suggest movement and freedom to most people, but if you were in a serious auto accident when you were young, cars may represent pain or danger to you. Trust your own instincts and intuition—after all, the cards and your subconscious are attempting to communicate with you, and they will do it in imagery that you can understand.

*"The true Tarot is symbolism; it speaks no other language and offers no other signs."*
—ARTHUR EDWARD WAITE, *THE PICTORIAL KEY TO THE TAROT*

# Chapter 4

# NUMEROLOGY AND THE TAROT

Numerology—the spiritual study of numbers—is thousands of years old. Esoteric traditions have long honored and understood the symbology of numbers. Each number has a sacred, "secret" meaning as well as a mundane one, and each possesses its own special characteristics.

A typical tarot deck's Minor Arcana (we'll talk more about the Minor Arcana as we go along) contains four suits with ten numbered cards in each suit, just like our everyday playing cards do. In the tarot, however, numbers don't just denote quantities—(a nine doesn't beat a six, for instance)—they serve as important symbols and keys to interpreting a reading.

The tarot's numbered cards, also called pips, have individual meanings based on the resonance of the number. The numbers also show stages of development and, as such, link each pip to other numbered cards that appear in a reading. Later, when we delve more deeply into the Minor Arcana, we'll also consider the relationships between numbers and suits. The cards of the Major Arcana also bear numbers, and we'll talk about those too. For now, let's take a cursory look at what the numbers on the cards can tell us.

| A QUICK KEY TO NUMBERS AND THEIR MEANINGS | |
|---|---|
| **Number** | **Meaning** |
| Ace | Beginnings, individuality, focus |
| Two | Partnership, union, balance/imbalance |
| Three | Self-expression, development, reaping benefits |
| Four | Stability, work, perseverance |
| Five | Change, instability, stress |
| Six | Contentment, harmony, community |
| Seven | Retreat, spirituality, inner growth |
| Eight | Material gain, recognition, success |
| Nine | Humanitarianism, wisdom, completion |
| Ten | Endings and beginnings, fulfillment |

*"Those who deepen themselves in what is called in the Pythagorean sense 'the study of numbers' will learn through the symbolism of numbers to understand life and the world."*

—RUDOLF STEINER, FOUNDER OF ANTHROPOSOPHY

AND THE WALDORF SCHOOLS

# ACE (ONE)

The number one signifies a beginning. The ace shows that a seed has been planted and something has begun to sprout, though you may not know how it will develop yet. Aces are full of potential—the time is ripe with possibilities, and you have the choice to initiate something. When an ace appears in your reading, it says you're at a starting point; you're being offered a new opportunity. It's up to you to follow through—it won't automatically happen.

Drawing an ace can indicate being alone. Sometimes you need solitude to nurture a new idea, project, or experience before going public with it. Aces also can show focus, concentrated energy, and clarity of purpose as you move toward your goal.

Notice that each of the aces in the Rider-Waite-Smith deck shows a disembodied hand extending from a cloud, holding out the "tool" to the seeker. When an ace turns up in a reading, you're being offered an opportunity, a gift from the Goddess.

# TWO

The number two depicts a union or partnership, with another person, a spiritual entity, or two parts of yourself. When a two comes up in a reading, it can mean you're forming an alliance of some sort—or want to. Two also represents balance; it may show you're balancing polarities in your life or that you need to correct an imbalance.

Because the number two follows the ace, it can also suggest development in whatever you started with the ace. This may mean expanding, stabilizing, or splintering your efforts. Perhaps joining forces with someone can help you achieve your objective.

# THREE

Three is the number of self-expression and communication; it represents expansion, optimism, and development. The seed you planted with the ace—a project, idea, relationship, or course of action—now starts to take form. When you draw a three in a reading, it indicates you're opening up, moving beyond your own little circle, and broadening your horizons.

## From Idea to Reality
We live in a three-dimensional world, and threes, in the tarot, represent self-expression and bringing ideas into reality. In spellwork, witches sometimes repeat an affirmation, incantation, or act three times to seal a spell and direct its physical manifestation.

Sometimes, however, the growth or development represented by the number three happens too fast. You may spread yourself too thin or max out your resources. Generally, drawing a three suggests a pleasant period when you feel happy and reap benefits—so long as you pay attention to what you're doing.

# FOUR

The number four represents foundation, stability, and security. When a four appears in a reading, it can indicate a time of self-discipline, work, and service, as well as putting down roots and establishing yourself. Organization and pragmatism are important now. You need clarity too, if you want a situation to turn out well.

If you're in a place where you want to be—a home, job, or relationship—the four advises you to focus on stabilizing yourself. If you're not satisfied with your current situation, it's time to plan and work at making constructive changes. Life can seem all work and no play now, but if your objectives are clear, you won't mind doing the work. Four's message is take things slow and steady; be patient as you endeavor to bring your dreams to fruition.

> *"The symbolism of four is drawn primarily from the square and the four-armed cross. The square was the emblem of the earth in both India and China. The four-armed cross is the most common emblem of totality, the four directions of space."*
> —JACK TRESIDDER, *THE COMPLETE DICTIONARY OF SYMBOLS*

# FIVE

Five is the number of freedom, change, instability, and curiosity. In a reading, fives suggest excitement, adventure, movement, and challenges afoot, but you might be in for a roller-coaster ride! Sometimes the changes seem to be happening too fast, causing stress and anxiety. Five's energy can be too much to handle, especially if you're a quiet, sensitive person. You might need to get some perspective and consider the risks involved instead of dashing ahead. "Take five" before you make an important decision.

# SIX

Six is the number of caring, compassion, and community. It signifies a period of calm after the storm, when you tend to everyday needs, rest, and establish harmony in your immediate surroundings. When six shows up in a reading, it's time to stop, catch your breath, and relish the rewards of your efforts. After a period of activity or stress, you can finally enjoy some ease. Misunderstandings can now be resolved harmoniously too. Six's vibration is cooperative, so it can represent working with others or providing service of some kind—just remember to take care of your own needs as well.

## Solomon's Seal

The six-pointed star or Seal of Solomon symbolizes harmony because it depicts the integration of feminine and masculine energies. In alchemy, the upward-pointing triangle signifies the male or yang force; the downward-pointing triangle represents the female or yin force. The two triangles are united in the seal.

# SEVEN

The number seven symbolizes the inner life, solitude, and soul-searching. When sevens appear in a reading, they indicate a time of turning inward to discover the meaning of life, what has happened to you and why. You may be searching, on a psychological or spiritual level, for answers.

Perhaps you feel a need to be alone, to retreat from the busyness of everyday life, to find your own true path. Spiritual or metaphysical subjects might interest you now. This isn't a good time to start or devote yourself to a material or financial undertaking, as your priorities lie elsewhere. In some cases, drawing a seven may mean you're spending too much time alone and need to socialize more.

## A Mystical Number

Seven is a mystical number that represents wisdom, spirituality, and wholeness—there are seven heavens, seven days of the week, seven colors in the visible spectrum, seven notes in a musical scale, and seven major chakras in the human body.

# EIGHT

Eight represents abundance, material prosperity, and worldly power. It's the number of leadership and authority. In a tarot reading, an eight says you possess the organizational and managerial skills for material success—or, conversely, that you need to develop them. Its appearance suggests it's time to get your financial or worldly affairs in order.

Eight's vibration is linked with honor, respect, awards, public recognition, and abundance in all areas of life. When you draw an eight, the potential for achieving these benefits is there, but you need sincerity and dedication to come out on top. Sometimes an eight cautions you to be careful with money or possessions, or points out issues you have around abundance—or the lack of it.

### Eight and Infinity

On the spiritual level, eight symbolizes cosmic consciousness—infinity's symbol is a figure eight turned on its side. Look at The Magician card in the Rider-Waite-Smith deck and you'll notice this symbol above the magus's head. Here it symbolizes wholeness, the development of multiple aspects of life—physical, mental, and spiritual. Witches also connect eight with the eight sabbats in the Wheel of the Year—you can see this wheel symbolized on the Wheel of Fortune card in the Rider-Waite-Smith deck.

# NINE

The number nine represents humanitarianism, compassion, and tolerance. It also signifies gaining wisdom through experience. Drawing a nine suggests you're dedicating yourself to helping others or to a worthy cause. The challenge is to not sacrifice your own well-being in the process. Nine's vibration allows you to see the big picture—you can give freely of yourself because you feel complete within yourself.

Because nine is the last single-digit number, it represents the end of a cycle. It's time to tie up loose ends. In most cases, nines depict fulfillment, completion, and the sense of satisfaction that comes from having reached a peak after a long, arduous climb. As such, nine symbolizes the bridge between the material and the spiritual realm.

# TEN

Ten represents both an ending and a beginning, the point of transition from the completed cycle to a new cycle. When tens show up in a reading, whatever you've been working on or have been involved with is over—you've gotten whatever you're likely to get out of it, and it's time to move on. That's good news if you've been going through a rough period. It also serves as an affirmation: You've done what you set out to do.

If you've been stagnating lately, drawing a ten tells you to challenge yourself and reach for a higher level. As happens in any period of transition, you may experience discomfort or anxiety about entering a new cycle. Even though you feel you're sitting on the fence, you know that "he who hesitates is lost." A ten in a reading says a decision must be made.

### Sign of Wholeness

Ten carries the symbolism of wholeness. The Kabbalah's Tree of Life features ten sephirot (emanations of divinity). In Judeo-Christian teaching, God gave ten commandments to Moses. Ten represented the whole of creation in the Pythagorean system, depicted as a figure called the *tetraktys*, made up of ten points divided into four rows.

*The Modern Witchcraft Book of Tarot*

# Chapter 5

# USING THE TAROT

People often ask me, "How can a deck of cards reveal the future?" My reply is simple: by revealing yourself to you. As we said earlier, tarot cards, like dreams, contain meaningful symbols that trigger your intuition. They expand your vision and let you see what lies beyond the limits of ordinary reality. They provide a convenient way to get at the inner truth of a situation. They speak to the creative part of your mind, the part that serves as the architect of your life, to help you make informed choices and design your future the way you want it to be.

## YES, YOU REALLY ARE PSYCHIC

Everyone is psychic. You've probably received a phone call and known who was on the other end even before you looked at caller ID. Maybe you've had other experiences of knowing things you couldn't explain in ordinary terms. Some people find that scary, but you shouldn't let it worry you. We're given this ability to help us navigate the choppy waters of life on earth. Your sixth sense is as natural as the other five—sight, hearing, taste, smell, and touch—and just as valuable.

Some of us are naturally more gifted than others at using our sixth sense, just as some of us have more native musical talent or athletic ability. As is true with music or athletics, the more you practice, the stronger your psychic muscles will become. However, first you must take the tarot—and yourself—seriously. Fear will block results; so will a frivolous attitude. Keep an open mind. Trust the insights you receive. Let the cards speak directly to your inner self. Tune in to what you *feel* about each card. The interpretations given in this book are useful, but they're only guides, not "facts" carved in stone. Your own interpretations are what count.

---

### Find Your Own Perspective

Lara Houston of the International Tarot Foundation explains that when the same question is presented to a group of students, "They each read for the question and yet they are likely to lay different cards to each other. The interesting part of this is that mostly all will reach the same outcome and give similar guidance. This indicates that we each use our own perspective and understanding of language to interpret."

---

Here's a quick exercise you can try, before you start studying the interpretations presented in Part II of this book. Pick one card from the deck. Take a few moments to look at it, without analyzing what you see—just let impressions bubble up in your mind. Jot down in your tarot journal or book of shadows what you feel or sense in connection with the card. Then look up the usual meaning of the card and see how much of what you sensed matches. (If your take was completely different, that's okay too.)

# THE STEPS IN A TAROT READING

If you've never treated yourself to a tarot reading with a professional, you may want to give it a try—it can be very informative. However, because this book is about learning to do it yourself, I'm going to share with you some basic features of a typical tarot reading. Remember, though, each reader will approach a reading in his or her own unique way—and so will you when you've developed an understanding of the tarot.

## *Preparing Yourself for a Reading*

Before you do a reading for yourself or consult with a professional tarot reader, determine your main concerns and/or your reasons for seeking advice. I find it helps to write down your question(s) or the

*The Modern Witchcraft Book of Tarot*

situation(s) foremost in your mind at the time of the reading. Additionally, here are some other things you can do in preparation for a reading:

- Turn off the TV; silence your phone. Make sure you won't be disturbed during the course of your reading. Post a sign on the door, if need be: *Do Not Disturb.*
- Choose a place to work where you feel comfortable and safe. You may want to cleanse the space by smudging it with burning sage or incense or using another method you prefer. Witches may want to bring out their brooms and sweep away "bad vibes" or disruptive energies.
- If you wish, light candles, hold a favorite crystal, chant, pray, play soothing music—do whatever helps you calm body and mind, so you can step outside your ordinary, everyday world into sacred space.
- Meditate on your question/concern for a few minutes. This relaxes you, centers your mind, and enables you to let go of distractions that could interfere with your reading.
- If you feel a connection with a spirit guide, angel, deity, animal guardian, or other entity, you may wish to invite that being to assist you in the reading.

### Choosing a Significator

At the beginning of a reading, you usually select a card to represent you (or the person for whom the reading is being done, if you're reading for someone else). This card is known as a significator, and it brings you into the reading symbolically.

Because the court cards (the kings, queens, knights, and pages, which we'll talk about soon) often depict people, they are popular choices for significators. You might select a card that corresponds to your sex, age, and astrological sign. It may also tie in with your profession, interests, physical characteristics, and other personal factors.

> *"[The court cards] represent the anima and animus, the female and male attributes of the elements. The court cards also represent stages of maturity. Depending on the suit and level of maturity, a court card represents a combination of element and personality."*
>
> —SUSAN LEVITT, *INTRODUCTION TO TAROT*

We'll talk more about significators in Part III when we look at laying out cards in "spreads" to do readings. In Chapters 11 and 12, we'll also discuss other matters related to doing readings.

## Shuffling the Cards

Shuffling a tarot pack does more than simply mix up the cards and rearrange them for your reading. It also transfers your personal energy to the cards. That's why it's a good idea to cleanse the cards each time a different person touches them. One easy way to do this is to hold the deck in the smoke of burning sage or incense for a few moments. I recommend keeping one deck for yourself and using another one when you do readings for other people. After you (or the person for whom you're reading) has finished shuffling, cut the cards. I usually ask my clients to blow on the cards before cutting them—as if they are breathing "life" into the deck.

### Querent

The person for whom a tarot reading is being done, the one who seeks answers to his or her questions, is called a querent.

## Laying Out the Cards

A tarot reading usually involves laying out a number of cards in a particular pattern, known as a spread. The position a card occupies in the spread means something special—usually in relationship to the other cards in the spread. As you'll see in Part III, different spreads have different purposes. A reader interprets not only the card itself but also its placement in the pattern, its role in the big picture. A reading may be as simple as drawing a single card, or it may include every card in the deck—or even require laying out several different spreads.

### Record Your Readings

If a card seems especially unrelated to your question, look at it several times during the day, recording in your journal or grimoire any feelings it stirs in you. Before bed, review the card and your notes. If you have a dream that is influenced by the images on the card, record it also. Often dreams comment on your daily readings.

# OTHER WAYS TO USE TAROT CARDS

Most of us consult the tarot to gain insight into our life situations, for guidance and direction when making decisions, or to see what the future holds for us. But those aren't the only ways you can use the tarot.

## Meditating with Tarot Cards

Tarot cards are wonderful aids to meditation and contemplation. Their thought-provoking imagery can help to focus your mind. Choose a card that represents a situation or condition you seek, such as Temperance or Strength. Gaze at the symbols on the card and allow your mind to reflect upon their meanings. You may want to display one or more cards on your altar or in another place where you'll see them often, to remind you of an intention or for inspiration.

## Spellworking with Tarot Cards

Tarot cards can also serve as powerful visual aids in spellcraft. If you do magick work, you already know that vivid imagery enhances your spells and rituals.

- You can designate a card to represent you in a spell or ritual.
- You can select a card that depicts an outcome you desire and incorporate it into a spell.
- You can include cards in talismans and amulets.
- If you know feng shui, you can position a card in a prescribed place in your home to help bring about conditions you seek.

The possibilities are endless. In Part IV, you'll find lots of spells that use tarot cards in a variety of ways for love, prosperity, protection, and other purposes.

## Keeping a Tarot Journal

As you venture down this path, I recommend you keep a tarot journal. Here you can jot down your thoughts and impressions about the cards, note things you read in books or online that pique your interest, and record insights you gain along the way.

Keep track of the readings you do for yourself too. In my journal, I date each entry and write down the question I asked or the concern for which I sought advice. Then I sketch the spread I laid out in response to my question or concern. I describe what the reading means to me at the time, anything else that seems relevant or anything I'm still unclear about. Later, I can come back and revisit the reading and compare that to what transpired.

One of the main reasons we turn to the tarot, of course, is to learn what the future holds for us. If you want to build your predictive skills, try using the cards to "see" the outcome of something that you will know tomorrow, such as the winner of a ballgame or a political election. Keep track of your "hits." Over time, your success rate will likely improve.

---

### Shaping Your Insight

Lara Houston of the International Tarot Foundation taught herself the tarot by journaling—and in the process established a special communication with her deck of cards. "I had a Facebook group of 2,000 members (non-readers) and I gave readings all day long. I would 'talk' to my deck, asking questions on certain cards and insights. I realized I was shaping the insight of my cards too . . . Over a period of journaling free readings, myself and my deck developed an understanding where my perspective and understanding of language became the insights of my cards."

---

## Caring for Your Cards

Before you handle your deck, wash your hands thoroughly in warm water, preferably with a fragrance-free, natural, pure soap. Soap made from glycerin or vegetable oils is the best because it contains no animal products.

Store your cards carefully when they're not in use. Many people wrap their decks in silk because silk is believed to possess special protective qualities that prevent the cards from becoming tainted by ambient energetic vibrations. Some companies make beautiful velvet, satin, and tapestry pouches—with zippers or drawstrings—specially designed to hold tarot cards. You can also store your deck in an attractive wooden box.

Between readings, stash your cards in a private place—you'll always know where they are when you want them, and you can be sure they won't fall into the wrong hands. Care for your cards as you would any treasure or valued magickal tool, and they will serve you well.

# PART II

# Interpreting *the* Cards

# Chapter 6

# THE SUIT OF WANDS

Fan out the cards in the suit of wands and look at them for a few minutes. You'll probably notice that the people on these cards (assuming you're using a storytelling deck) appear to be having a good time at whatever they're doing. Even the folks on the challenging cards—the Five, Seven, and Ten—seem quite capable of handling the tasks at hand.

As discussed in Chapter 3, we connect the wands with creativity, enthusiasm, inspiration, self-expression, adventure, drive, zest for life, and activity in the outer world. These cards show how you express your talents, how you approach challenges in life, and your potential for success. Often they represent the work you do, either your career or an avocation about which you feel passionately, such as art or music. Wands go by various names in different decks—rods, staves, batons—and artists depict them in many colorful ways—as wooden staffs, poles, tree branches sprouting flowers or leaves, scepter-like rods, or flaming torches.

However they're pictured, wands are obvious phallic symbols. That's because they're linked with the masculine force in the universe. They also represent the element of fire and correspond to the suit of clubs in an ordinary playing deck.

---

### Baseball Tarot

You can find a tarot deck to suit almost anyone's interests. For example, the Baseball Tarot depicts wands as—you guessed it—baseball bats.

---

# KING OF WANDS

*Keywords: Leadership, self-confidence, success, good fortune, loyalty*

As befits a king, the King of Wands often appears seated on a throne, wearing a handsome robe and a crown. He's a dignified man who exudes confidence, authority, and power, yet he doesn't seem at all threatening. In fact, he's usually shown as a handsome and benevolent ruler. In a reading, the King may signify an actual person. When he does, it's generally a mature man who's obtained a position of wealth and status—perhaps the head of a business or a leader in the community.

---

### Which Way Does the King Face?

In some decks, the King faces sideways, and whether he is looking toward or away from other cards in a spread will have a bearing on the reading.

---

### *Upright*

The King upright is a fortunate card, regardless of the situation. If he represents a real person, it's someone you can trust and rely on to do the right thing. He's a loyal friend, a fair-minded employer, a wise adviser, a competent and honest leader. This intelligent man has high ideals. He's an active, energetic, independent individual with a passion for life and an adventurous nature.

- In a reading about money, you can expect good things to come your way when the King appears. Sometimes the King means getting a raise, that a venture will pay off, or that you have financial support.
- If the reading is about your job, success is assured. The King may indicate a promotion or recognition for your efforts. It can also show you moving into a position of authority. Now is a good time to take a chance, for victory is yours.

*The Modern Witchcraft Book of Tarot*

- In a question about love, the King of Wands says the relationship is a strong one with plenty of affection and passion, perhaps between two lively, creative, outgoing people.

## Reversed

When the King of Wands is reversed, you may run into delays or your success isn't as great as you'd hoped for. If he represents a real person, it may be someone who's not available to you or who can't help you even if he wants to. Perhaps his loyalties lie elsewhere. He's probably not dishonest or irresponsible, but he may not be forthcoming.

- In a reading about money, the King reversed can mean you have to wait for money that's due to you or you won't receive as much as you would've liked.
- In a job-related matter, he can mean a project will take longer than you'd planned or you'll have to work harder than you'd expected. Perhaps some of the most creative aspects of an undertaking will get nixed by higher-ups.
- If you asked about a relationship, this King can indicate waning enthusiasm. Or, a romance may be slow getting started. Sometimes it shows a person who's committed to another.

---

### Bully Card

In the extreme, the reversed King of Wands can be the "bully card." As Mary K. Greer writes in *The Complete Book of Tarot Reversals*, "You might oppose others simply as a display of one-upmanship. You can be aggressive and abuse others, like a bully or a commandant with no humanity."

---

# QUEEN OF WANDS

*Keywords: Creativity, passion, prosperity, fruitfulness, generosity*

Like the King, the Queen of Wands is often pictured seated on a throne, wearing an elegant robe and a crown. She's usually a beautiful mature woman who epitomizes feminine authority, confidence, warmth, and enthusiasm. In a reading, the Queen may signify an actual person. When she does, it's someone who's active, vibrant, and outgoing, perhaps a woman with a creative nature.

---

### Brigid the Goddess

The Queen of Wands bears similarities to the Celtic goddess Brigid, who rules both the hearth and the forge. Often she's pictured stirring a fiery cauldron, symbolic of creativity and inspiration. Witches link Brigid with self-expression, smithcraft, and healing and celebrate her sabbat, known as Imbolc, on February 1.

---

## *Upright*

A fortunate card, the upright Queen gives you a "thumbs up." If this card signifies a real person, she's a figure who commands respect—whether she's in the boardroom or the home. A wise adviser, she is also a loyal friend, a loving partner, a trustworthy authority. She has a nurturing, colorful, and generous nature; she's confident in her abilities and encourages others to do their best. Like the King, she may play a prominent role in a business or her community.

- In a question about money, the Queen says, "Do what you love; the money will follow." You may receive money from a creative venture or prosper through a partnership or other alliance.
- If you asked about a job matter, the upright Queen shows a period of fulfillment, when a project bears fruit and you're happy with the outcome. This is also a good time to birth or expand a venture.

- In a reading about a relationship, she shows a passionate romance between loyal, loving partners.

*"The Queen of Wands represents a vital, passionate and aggressive female who wants to help other people through her efforts. Though she appears to be fighting those who cross her path, she is a true champion of those she supports."*

—NANCY SHAVICK, THE TAROT:<br>A GUIDE TO READING YOUR OWN CARDS

## Reversed

When the Queen of Wands is reversed, she can mean a situation won't come to fruition as fast as you'd hoped or your satisfaction will be limited. Your enthusiasm may flag or you just don't feel inspired. If she's a real person, she's a powerful, emotional woman who demands respect and absolute loyalty. She can be jealous and manipulative, both in love and in business—don't cross her. This is the "drama queen" card.

- In a reading about money, the reversed Queen warns you to be careful with investments or business spending—particularly in joint ventures.
- If you've asked about a job-related issue, she may indicate deception or power struggles. Watch your back; a coworker may not be trustworthy.
- In a relationship reading, she may suggest emotional upsets, infidelity, or a cooling of affection.

# KNIGHT OF WANDS

*Keywords: Adventure, travel, excitement, movement, restlessness*

KNIGHT of WANDS.

In the tarot, knights are traditionally shown on horseback, armored, like the knights of old. Some decks call them princes or knaves; the Motherpeace deck calls them sons. Knights are messengers and travelers. The Knight of Wands is an energetic young man, sometimes seated on a rearing horse, and he appears to be ready to ride off into the wild blue yonder—or perhaps to a jousting match. In a reading, the Knight may signify an actual person. If so, he's a lively, fun-loving adventurer, a daredevil, perhaps an athlete.

---

### A Horse of a Different Color

The Knight of Wands reminds us of the days when knights jousted with wooden rods, practicing for battle. Different decks portray the Knight's horse in different colors—reddish-gold in the Rider-Waite-Smith deck, black in the Thoth Tarot—and the color holds symbolic meaning. Often the animal charges, prances, or rears up on its back legs to depict the gusto represented by this card.

---

## Upright

When the Knight of Wands appears upright, he brings good news. Sometimes he represents a trip or relocation. Some sort of movement or activity is afoot, of a happy kind. If the Knight represents a real person, he's a good-natured and likable chap, generous of spirit, idealistic, a loyal friend.

- In a reading about money, he suggests a fortunate opportunity is on the horizon and/or a financial change is coming. You may receive money unexpectedly. Or, the card may advise you to take a financial risk.

*The Modern Witchcraft Book of Tarot*

- In a reading about work, the Knight upright may represent a promotion or a transfer to another locale/company. He can also point to a business trip in the near future.
- If you asked about love, this Knight indicates an enthusiastic and enjoyable affair, but don't expect it to last. Have fun, but realize your partner is a free spirit who doesn't like commitments.

## Reversed

When the Knight of Wands is reversed, a message (or paperwork) may be delayed or an event postponed. If he represents a real person, this card cautions that the message—or the messenger—may not be reliable. That includes social media; check out those Facebook posts before you share them.

- In a reading about money, the reversed Knight advises you not to take a financial risk now. Or, it can mean you're spending more than you can afford, maybe on a car or trip. Tuck those credit cards away before you get in trouble.
- If you asked about a work-related matter, the Knight reversed can indicate restlessness or a job change. Sometimes it shows canceling or postponing a business trip.
- In a question about love, this card shows fickleness, flirtatiousness, and lack of trust. One person (or both) doesn't want to settle down. Sometimes a relationship ends or a romantic event (maybe a vacation) gets postponed.

# PAGE OF WANDS

*Keywords: Questing, playfulness, innocence, curiosity, learning*

The Page of Wands is a youthful figure, sometimes a boy, sometimes a girl. Older decks often show him or her in Renaissance-style court garb with short pants and stockings, but in contemporary decks, he or she may wear regular kids' clothing. The page goes by other names too, depending on the deck, including child, daughter, and apprentice. The Collective Tarot calls them seekers. In a reading, the Page of Wands may signify an actual person; if so, it's a spunky child or young person who's full of curiosity and eager to learn.

### Upright

The Page of Wands represents the early stages of a situation or undertaking. It shows an optimistic attitude, enthusiasm, and an eagerness to succeed. If the card represents a person in your life, it could be a younger relative or friend, an apprentice, student, or assistant. This is the "student card." Sometimes it indicates a person with a childlike (or childish) nature, regardless of age.

- In a reading about money, this Page shows a new investment has the potential to pay off. The card can also recommend taking a creative approach to making money.
- In a reading about work, you're probably starting a new job you enjoy, learning a new skill, or preparing yourself for a career of a creative nature.
- If you asked about love, this card indicates an innocent and playful approach to a relationship. It shows openness, honesty, and an optimistic attitude toward love.

*The Modern Witchcraft Book of Tarot*

## Reversed

Reversed, the Page of Wands represents a delay, mix-up, or disappointment. Sometimes it says the time isn't right to start something or that you're on the wrong track. If the card signifies a real person, it may mean he or she can't be trusted or isn't up to the task.

- In a reading about money, the reversed Page advises caution. Seek advice from someone more knowledgeable and experienced. Wait a while and get more info before laying down your hard-earned cash.
- If you asked about work, this card suggests you may be naive about a situation related to your job. Or, it may show you need to learn more, develop your skills, or put in more effort to get ahead.
- In a reading about love, this Page can show childish behavior, hang-ups from childhood that interfere with the relationship, unrealistic expectations, or lack of commitment.

---

### Page or Princess?

In medieval times, a page served as an assistant to a knight or a nobleman, and sometimes as a court messenger. Although those pages were boys, and in early tarot packs they're portrayed as youthful males, contemporary decks often depict them as young females to establish a gender balance among the court cards. The Thoth Tarot, for example, calls these cards princesses.

---

# ACE OF WANDS

*Keywords: Opportunity, inspiration, adventure, creativity, a new start*

Aces signify beginnings. They also represent focused energy and clear, singular intent. In the Rider-Waite-Smith tarot and some other decks, the Ace of Wands shows a disembodied hand emerging from a cloud, grasping a stick from which new shoots grow. The message: Here's an opportunity; grab it. Some decks picture only a wand, often one that's large and elaborate, like a ruler's scepter or a witch's ceremonial tool.

---

### Highest or Lowest

In modern-day games of chance, the ace often stands as the highest card. In the tarot, however, it occupies the other end of the spectrum—not the lowest, but the earliest step.

---

## *Upright*

This Ace symbolizes a new beginning, one full of passion and rich with promise. You're ready to express yourself in a new, dynamic way. You want to be seen in a new light. You're bringing your creativity to bear in an exciting endeavor, and you're psyched about the possibilities opening up before you. I think of this as the "go for it card."

- In a reading about money, this Ace suggests profits coming from a creative venture. It can also mean you're investing your resources and energy in a new enterprise you feel passionate about.
- In a reading about work, the card shows you expressing yourself passionately through a creative endeavor, perhaps even forging a new identity. You're totally focused on your objective, and your enthusiasm will help bring success.

*The Modern Witchcraft Book of Tarot*

- In a reading about a relationship, the Ace promises new love of a highly romantic, joyful, and passionate kind. It can also mean loyalty, commitment, and a strong sense of purpose—perhaps of a creative nature—in an existing partnership.

*"You are always nearer to the divine and the true sources of your power than you think. The lure of the distant and the difficult is deceptive. The great opportunity is where you are . . . Every place is under the stars, every place is the center of the world."*
—JOHN BURROUGHS, *STUDIES IN NATURE AND LITERATURE*

## Reversed

Delays and complications have stalled an endeavor, and you feel frustrated or impatient. As a result, you may question yourself and your ability. You might have to rethink your plans and make adjustments, or perhaps sit back and wait for a better time.

- In a reading about money, this card suggests consolidating your finances and focusing on what's essential. Curb spending—don't overextend yourself now.
- In a reading about work, it can mean an enthusiastic start fizzled or met with obstacles. You don't have to give up, but you may need to put in some extra effort or reassess the situation. This card may advise you to wait for a more auspicious time, when the force is with you, to begin a project or other venture.
- In a reading about love, the Ace reversed suggests an enjoyable relationship may be short-lived. Perhaps you approached an affair wearing rose-colored glasses and now see it's not what you really want. This card may also mean the initial passion in a romance is dwindling.

# TWO OF WANDS

*Keywords: Developing goals, involvement in a creative project, taking action, choices*

This card shows you taking action to accomplish something you feel passionately about: a creative project, a business, or an adventure. You may have to make a choice between two options or bring two factors together to achieve success.

## Upright

You're beginning to assert yourself, taking charge of an endeavor. Upright, the Two shows you waiting to see results in a venture. You feel confident of your success. You may accept advice or assistance from someone else, but you won't compromise your position or leadership.

- In a reading about money, this card indicates you may benefit from other people's guidance, ideas, and encouragement but want to make it on your own, rather than depending on others.
- In a reading about work, the Two shows you investing lots of energy in an endeavor. Take charge and don't let other people stand in your way, dissuade you, or diminish your enthusiasm.
- In a reading about love, the Two upright suggests you're building a rewarding partnership. Sometimes it represents a creative relationship in which two people inspire and encourage each other.

## Reversed

When the Two of Wands is reversed, it can indicate a delay or difficulty. You may be in for a surprise that requires you to make changes. Perhaps someone you relied on or believed in disappoints you.

- If you asked about money, this card may mean financing for a project gets delayed, or an investment doesn't produce the return you'd hoped for. Use caution in financial partnerships or contracts.

- In a reading about work, the reversed Two can mean you'll have to work harder than you'd expected to bring your dream to fruition. Sometimes it indicates you've gotten off track and need to take action to control a situation. You may have to rein in a colleague or contractor, or another person may not hold up his or her end.
- In a reading about love, this card advises being upfront and honest with your partner. If the relationship is rocky, you may have to make adjustments, especially if you've been too dependent or detached in the past.

# THREE OF WANDS

*Keywords: Creativity and skill, self-expression, growth, competence, manifestation*

Now is the time to show the world what you can do. You've worked hard to develop your talents and have confidence in your abilities. You feel passionately about what you do and believe you can inspire others. Express yourself.

### Upright

You've developed a project, business, creative endeavor, or other venture, and now you're ready to share it with others. By devoting yourself fully to your goal, you can succeed. Do what's necessary to bring your dreams to fruition.

- In a reading about money, the upright Three shows increase and financial support coming to you. You may have to spend money to make money, but this card promises success.
- In a reading about work, this card suggests an exciting time when your efforts start to bear fruit. You're giving it your all, inspiring others, and attracting people who are eager to help you. Your ideas begin to take form. Collaboration can be beneficial.

- If you asked about a relationship, the Three indicates a commitment—an engagement or marriage. You and a partner express passionate feelings for each other and celebrate your love.

*"Hidden alliances work to move you into your authentic vocation as soon as you begin to commit to it."*
—RICK JAROW, *CREATING THE WORK YOU LOVE*

## Reversed

You still have work to do before you go public with your ideas. Perhaps you could benefit from honing your skills. Some areas of an undertaking still need clarification, or you may need to win the support and blessing of others in order to advance.

- In a question about money, this card can mean the financial support you need isn't there at this time. You might have to work extra hard for a while to make ends meet—be prudent in spending.
- In a reading about work, the reversed Three suggests you're not ready yet to market your project/ideas. You feel passionately about what you're doing, but you still have to convince other people to get onboard. For artistic people, this card advises, "Don't give up your day job yet."
- In a reading about love, you may feel strongly about a partner but aren't ready yet to make a commitment. Or, the other person may not be as emotionally invested as you are.

# FOUR OF WANDS

*Keywords: Success, comfort, prosperity, reaping rewards, celebration*

An extremely positive card, the Four of Wands signifies happiness, success, comfort, and security. You've used your energy and talents wisely and worked hard—now you're reaping the rewards due to you. In the Rider-Waite-Smith deck, the wands are festooned with garlands of fruit and flowers. It's time to relax and enjoy life.

## Upright

Everything is working out well when this card comes up in a reading. It indicates pleasure and prosperity, financial stability, and a happy home life. I call this the "comfort card." You've shown the world who you are and what you can achieve, and you've gained the recognition and rewards you deserve.

### The Harvest Card

In the Rider-Waite-Smith deck, the Four of Wands shows a happy couple celebrating, raising bouquets of flowers in the air. What we assume is their castle rises in the background; in the foreground, a gateway of sorts, decked with fruit and flowers, bids us enter and take part in the fun. This is a harvest card, one that witches might associate with the Midsummer sabbat, when we enjoy the fruits of our labors and rejoice in the earth's abundance.

- In a reading about money, the Four upright suggests prosperity and financial security. You may reap benefits from investments or make money from the sale of property.
- In a reading about work, this card shows success, harmony, and stability in your business or career. You derive satisfaction from a job well done. The Four also represents happiness and fulfillment in a creative venture and perhaps recognition on a broader scale.

- In a reading about love, you find contentment, peace, and ease in a relationship. A happy and comfortable home life is yours.

*"We carry within us the wonders we seek without us."*
—Sir Thomas Browne, *Religio Medici*

## Reversed

Even when the Four of Wands is reversed, it's still a positive card. You may celebrate your good fortune with less fanfare, or your success may be more modest than if the card were upright. Still you're content with what you've accomplished and feel good about yourself.

- In a reading about money, the reversed Four finds you financially secure but says you shouldn't be extravagant or frivolous with your money.
- In a reading about work, you're in a solid, secure position and content with your creative output, though you may not be able to rest on your laurels yet. For the most part, cooperation exists in your business or workplace and you feel things are moving along satisfactorily—although, perhaps, not as quickly as you'd expected.
- In a reading about love, this card says you can resolve problems now. With a little effort, a pleasant and harmonious relationship is possible. Sometimes the reversed Four means a celebration gets delayed temporarily.

# FIVE OF WANDS

*Keywords: Competition, ego battles, disagreements, confusion*

When the Five of Wands appears, it suggests a struggle for power, money, or recognition. Ego battles may interfere with the smooth flow of life. In some cases, it shows competition for resources or control. Confusion and disagreements exist.

## *Upright*

Bickering and self-interest cause irritation, and you need to concern yourself with getting matters back on track. Discontent may arise from differences in philosophy or personality. When this card shows up, you may be defending your territory, putting up a fight to hold on to what you think is "yours." Try to assess the situation objectively—this may be a mock battle or a conflict of egos that lacks genuine substance.

- In a reading about money, this card may show your financial situation is unstable or competition is cutting into your take. Arguments about money and spending cause tension.
- In a reading about work, the Five can represent competition in the marketplace. In-house conflicts or stubbornness may also cause problems. Perhaps you're confused about your direction or you lack self-confidence.
- In a reading about love, this card suggests you're letting your ego rule. You may stubbornly refuse to compromise or make necessary changes. The Five can also reveal differences of perspective that cause problems.

## *Reversed*

It's time to adapt to challenging circumstances when the Five of Wands appears reversed. Old attitudes and behaviors need to be released. Seek a compromise; otherwise nobody wins. Don't get involved in questionable or risky practices at this time and be careful whom you trust.

- In a reading about money, the reversed Five can warn of losses due to confusion, stubbornness, unwise investments, or impracticality.
- In a reading about work, you're likely to experience lack of cooperation, bickering, and backbiting in your workplace. Competition may be fierce or underhanded. Seek higher ground and hold to your principles.
- In a reading about love, you need to be more flexible and resolve disputes. Both people are probably being selfish and self-centered. Try to see the other person's point of view.

# SIX OF WANDS

*Keywords: Victory, success, recognition, satisfaction*

The Six of Wands is the "victory card." You've faced challenges, won the fight, and deserve the accolades you receive. Success and good fortune are yours.

### Upright
The Six of Wands promises a time of happiness and fulfillment. You've marshaled your energies during times of struggle and overcome obstacles. Now you're on top and can expect recognition and rewards. You feel good about yourself and your accomplishments. Sometimes this card shows recovery from an illness or setback.

- In a reading about money, you can expect financial success. A long-term investment may pay off now or you may receive a raise/bonus.
- In a reading about work, this card can mean getting a promotion, receiving respect for your efforts, or seeing a creative project come to fruition. Enjoy your well-deserved success.

*The Modern Witchcraft Book of Tarot*

- In a reading about love, the upright Six indicates a time of happiness, love, and cooperation in a relationship. If you're seeking a partner, this card offers encouragement for true love.

## Card of Triumph

The Thoth Tarot labels the Six of Wands "Victory." The Rider-Waite-Smith deck shows a triumphant horseman riding at the head of a jubilant procession. Salvador Dali, however, takes a different approach in his deck; his horseman rides alone, signifying an inner conquest rather than besting an opponent in the outer world.

## *Reversed*

When the Six of Wands is reversed, it can mean you still have work to do before you can enjoy the success and happiness you seek. You may feel frustrated, but if you continue fighting for what you want, you should win. Sometimes this card suggests reassessing your goals.

- In a reading about money, this card can signify delays in getting money that's due to you or that an investment won't pay off as you'd expected.
- In a reading about work, the Six reversed indicates some struggles may exist in your workplace. Perhaps egos are getting in the way of cooperation, or you don't feel you get the recognition you deserve.
- In a reading about love, this card can mean you and your partner have some issues to work out before harmony can reign. If you're looking for love, you may have to wait a while longer.

# SEVEN OF WANDS

*Keywords: Courage, fighting for what you believe in, facing challenges*

When the Seven of Wands appears in a reading, you may need to stand up for yourself and fight for what you believe in. Challenges confront you, but you possess the resources to succeed. I think of this as the "don't give up card."

## *Upright*

When this card appears, you may need to fend off competitors or enemies to achieve your objective. Even if the challenges are formidable, you can overcome them. The Seven encourages you to stay strong and focus your will to win the struggle.

- In a reading about money, this card tells you to hold firm in a financial matter even if things appear difficult at present. Avoid arguments about money or possessions.
- In a reading about work, the upright Seven advises holding your ground. Try to keep your spirits up and don't show weakness. Keep working diligently for what you want—don't let other people distract you.
- In a reading about love, this card recommends trying to work things out with a partner instead of squabbling. It may seem easier to just give up, but if you keep a positive attitude you can resolve difficulties.

*"When you come to the end of your rope, tie a knot and hang on."*
—Franklin D. Roosevelt

## *Reversed*

The reversed Seven of Wands signifies a time of confusion. You can't decide how to handle a challenge or which direction to take to accomplish your objective. Lack of clarity may sap your willpower and make you feel like giving up.

*The Modern Witchcraft Book of Tarot*

- In a reading about money, competitors or unexpected expenses may cut into your financial resources. You may need to set firm guidelines for spending or seek assistance from someone else.
- In a reading about work, the Seven reversed cautions you to avoid problematic people and watch your back. Don't get into arguments with coworkers, bosses, or clients now. Choose your battles carefully.
- In a reading about love, this card indicates giving up on a relationship. You feel worn down by problems and don't know how to settle your differences. Counseling could help you gain clarity.

# EIGHT OF WANDS

*Keywords: Action, excitement, new experiences, urgency*

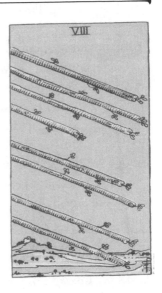

When the Eight of Wands appears, you can expect your life to speed up bigtime. This card suggests lots of action and excitement coming your way. This is the "carpe diem card." Whatever you've put into motion now takes off at a rapid pace. The Eight may also indicate a whirlwind trip.

### Upright

This card shows a busy period in your life, when you feel catapulted toward something you desire. Even though you may be a bit overwhelmed, you're excited and inspired, confident that all will turn out well. Take a few risks. Break out. Try new things and let go of what no longer suits you.

- In a reading about money, you may experience rapid gains or sudden opportunities. Perhaps you feel a sense of urgency in financial areas and may need to make split-second decisions.
- In a reading about work, the upright Eight suggests a time of inspiration, when things happen fast and you have to make quick decisions.

Your career moves forward rapidly and you have to hustle to keep up. This card can also represent job-related travel.

- In a reading about love, the upright Eight points to a passionate and exciting romance. It can indicate a sudden love affair that sweeps you off your feet or a hasty marriage.

### Reversed
When the Eight of Wands appears reversed, you may feel overwhelmed by the activity around you. Unexpected changes can throw you off balance. You may be required to travel or relocate, although you'd rather not. This card says, "Stop, world, I want to get off."

- In a reading about money, this card can mean money goes out faster than it comes in. Or, you may need to make financial decisions quickly.
- In a reading about your job, the reversed Eight indicates an exceptionally busy period when you have to work harder than usual. During this stressful time, you may feel unequal to the task. Perhaps you'll do lots of work-related traveling now.
- In a reading about love, a relationship seems to be happening too fast and you feel out of control. Sometimes this card can indicate an illicit, passionate affair.

# NINE OF WANDS
*Keywords: Courage, recovery, strength, success, conquest*

The Nine of Wands shows you defending your territory. You've demonstrated courage and tenacity and proved yourself to be a powerful force. Now you're in a strong position where you command respect, support, and rewards. This is also a card of recovery after a setback or illness.

## Upright

Nines represent completion and fulfillment, and when the Nine of Wands appears upright in a reading, it indicates you've finished a job and done it well. As a result of oppositions you've faced and triumphed over, you've grown stronger. You've demonstrated self-discipline, skill, and wisdom, and come out on top.

- In a reading about money, the upright Nine suggests you've suffered losses in the past but gotten matters in hand. Now you're in a more stable position.
- In a reading about work, this card says the worst is over. Stay the course; stand your ground. You've recovered from setbacks and success lies ahead.
- In a reading about love, the Nine shows you and a partner resolving difficulties. It promises happier times in your future. Perhaps you've both learned something important about yourselves and the relationship.

### Tie Knots

The last of the single-digit numbers, nine signifies fullness and power. As the result of three times three, it holds magickal symbolism in spellwork. To encourage the speed and effectiveness of an amulet or talisman, you can tie nine knots to close it. Chapter 15 contains a success spell that uses this method.

## Reversed

When the Nine of Wands appears reversed, it advises you to cut your losses and get out of a situation that isn't going to improve. You may be fighting a losing battle and need to move on to something else. Use the lessons you've learned as you chart a new course.

- In a reading about money, this card suggests an investment hasn't paid off. You need to stop throwing good money after bad. Perhaps you can benefit from establishing a budget or getting a handle on expenses.
- In a reading about work, the reversed Nine can signify a job change or even a new career path. You've accomplished as much as you can

in your current position. Seek a new direction that will rekindle your passion.

- In a reading about love, this card can indicate the end of a relationship. Perhaps an existing partnership has lost its glow or you've finished what you were meant to do together.

# TEN OF WANDS

*Keywords: Responsibility, strength, commitment, maturity, burdens, exhaustion*

The Ten of Wands shows you assuming responsibilities related to the new cycle that's beginning now. Although the task facing you seems more than you can bear, you have the strength to carry on and shoulder the burdens placed on you. Sometimes this card indicates exhaustion from taking on too much and pushing yourself too hard.

### Overburdened

Biddy Tarot (www.biddytarot.com) offers a nice interpretation of the image on this card in the Rider-Waite-Smith deck: "The Ten of Wands shows a man carrying a very heavy bundle of wands or sticks. He appears to be overburdened with the weight, yet he knows he is not far away from the town he is walking towards. This card appears to indicate someone who has just finished a harvest and is struggling to bring the fruits of his labours to the local market."

## Upright

The Ten of Wands suggests you've overextended yourself and you're weary from the effort. I think of this as the "carrying the world on your shoulders card." You may need to set boundaries or find a different way of handling the responsibilities you're struggling with. Are you carrying burdens that really don't belong to you? Where can you turn for help? Are you unwilling to give up control and stop insisting on doing everything yourself?

- In a reading about money, you may feel a pinch from taking on heavy obligations or supporting other people. Perhaps you've made unwise decisions and gotten into debt. Or, you may be staggering under the responsibilities of handling money, such as settling an estate.
- In a reading about work, this card suggests you've undertaken too much and you're burning out. Maybe you're working overtime or assuming someone else's duties as well as your own.
- In a reading about love, the Ten means taking a mature, responsible attitude toward a relationship. A card of commitment, it sometimes means supporting a partner through a difficult time.

### Reversed

When the Ten of Wands appears reversed, it can mean your burden is lifted and the responsibilities you've shouldered have lessened—perhaps because someone has pitched in to share the load. Because you've learned to delegate tasks and set boundaries for yourself, you have more freedom.

- In a reading about money, you may get a reprieve—an extension on a loan, a consolidation of debt, or another solution.
- In a reading about work, this card can show a lightening of your workload. Someone else may assume part of the responsibility, or pressure may ease due to outside factors.
- In a reading about love, a relationship may become more balanced or secure. If you've felt uncertain about a partner's commitment, now you know where you stand.

# Chapter 7

# THE SUIT OF CUPS

Spread out the cards in the suit of cups on a table or desktop and look at them for a few minutes. Because we associate this suit with emotions, you'll notice the people on the cards (assuming you're using a storytelling deck) appear involved in emotional situations—some happy, some sad. For example, some decks, including the Gilded Tarot and the Rider-Waite-Smith, show three joyful young women dancing on the Three of Cups; on the Five, a sorrowful person stands amid overturned chalices.

As we discussed in Chapter 3, cups not only describe emotions, they're also linked with intuition, creativity, nurturance, and relationships. Therefore, the cards in this suit frequently depict people in some kind of relationship. In a reading, cups indicate how you feel about something, how you express your feelings, how you interact with other people, how you care for yourself and others, and how you engage your creativity. Some decks call them chalices or other names, and artists depict them in various colorful ways—as ornate chalices, vases, cauldrons, bottles, bowls, vessels, wineglasses, and coffee mugs.

However they're pictured, cups are containers and symbolize the womb. That's because they're linked with the feminine force in the universe. They also represent the element of water and correspond to the suit of hearts in an ordinary playing deck. The chalice is one of the four primary tools in magick work.

# KING OF CUPS

*Keywords: Benevolence, culture, creativity, emotional warmth, protection*

In many decks, this King sits on a throne and wears rich garments and a crown. He usually appears as a benevolent authority, a father figure, who rules kindly and fairly. In a reading, the King of Cups may signify an actual person. When he does, it's generally a mature man who's cultured and knowledgeable in the arts.

### Upright

When the King of Cups appears upright, he represents strong emotions and creative talent. If he represents a real person, it's someone who wants to be loved and admired—he may go to great lengths to gain your attention and affection. Although he's easily hurt, he may not show it and can hold a grudge. He can be rather indulgent and controlling, but his friends can count on his support and protection.

- In a reading about money, the King can mean receiving money through a creative venture. Or, it may suggest your emotions are influencing a financial matter. Sometimes it represents a financial backer.
- If the reading is about your job, the King can describe a creative occupation. However, he may indicate you're longing for something better. Perhaps you've grown complacent.
- In a question about love, this card represents a deeply emotional, committed, and romantic relationship. It can suggest jealousy and possessiveness, however, or a need for more trust and openness.

### Reversed

The reversed King shows emotional turmoil, insecurity, and defensiveness. If he represents a real person, he can be manipulative, emotionally controlling, and vindictive. This card suggests dissatisfaction and frustration, perhaps because you aren't using your creativity.

- In a reading about money, the reversed King can show losses resulting from decisions made emotionally rather than rationally. Sometimes it indicates laziness, lack of direction, or an indulgent nature that lands you in debt.
- If the reading is about your job, this card suggests territorialism and power struggles. You may fear losing ground and try to control others. Secrecy, duplicity, and manipulation may exist in your workplace.
- In a question about love, the reversed King can mean fear of expressing love and caring. Jealousy, defensiveness, and/or emotional outbursts may cause problems. Perhaps you feel insecure in a partnership.

*"The King of Cups can be likened to Dionysus, the god of wine, poetry, and wild abandon, but who got drunk just once and, alone among the Greek gods, stayed faithful to his wife."*
—Mary K. Greer, *The Complete Book of Tarot Reversals*

---

# QUEEN OF CUPS

*Keywords: Creativity, fertility, strong emotion, change, intuition*

Usually the Queen of Cups appears seated on a throne, wearing a crown and lovely garments. A beautiful woman, she exudes warmth, sensuality, and maternal caring. In a reading, the Queen may signify an actual person. When she does, it's usually a mature woman who's creative, nurturing, changeable, intuitive, devoted as a wife or mother, and highly emotional; she is sometimes a "drama queen."

QUEEN of CUPS.

### Upright
The upright Queen represents deep emotions, compassion, and caring. When she comes up, you're experiencing strong feelings about someone or something. She can also urge you to use your intuition or

*The Modern Witchcraft Book of Tarot*

express your creativity. If this card signifies a real person, she's nurturing and generous, a mother figure. Ruled by her heart, not her head, she's changeable and sometimes unreliable.

*"The Queen of Cups is like a body of water, ever flowing onward as she brings inspiration and feeling to the world. Though she may sometimes seem as mutable as the sea itself, she is ever true to her heart."*
—Kris Waldherr, *The Lover's Path Tarot*

- In a reading about money, the Queen can mean earning money from a creative activity. Often she recommends being flexible and willing to make changes. Use your intuition as well as your intellect in financial matters.
- If the reading is about your job, this can be a creative and inspired time for you. To be happy, you need to be able to use your imagination in your job. Sometimes the Queen shows an unrealistic attitude about work or a desire to be taken care of rather than working.
- In a reading about love, the upright Queen represents a deeply romantic, sensual, and emotional relationship. You open yourself to a partner and lavish him or her with love. Sometimes the Queen advises you to be more discriminating. This is a fortunate card if you want to have children.

### Reversed

When the Queen appears reversed, you're letting your emotions rule you and you can't see a situation clearly. Either you're overly idealistic or you're shutting yourself off out of fear. If this card signifies a real person, she's probably manipulative, undependable, indiscriminate, or hypersensitive. This card may also show a situation is unstable.

- In a reading about money, the reversed Queen shows impracticality in money matters. You may spend more than you can afford on luxuries or are too generous with others. Sometimes this card says you shouldn't trust a financial adviser or business partner.
- If the reading is about your job, you may feel emotionally or creatively unfulfilled. Perhaps you're unrealistic about your abilities or

the demands of a job. The reversed Queen can also represent instability, bad feelings, or unsavory things going on behind the scenes in
your workplace.

- In a reading about love, this card can mean a relationship has soured.
Infidelity is possible. The reversed Queen can also show you or a
partner hiding your feelings—you need to be more open and trusting.

# KNIGHT OF CUPS

*Keywords: Communication, romance, travel,
idealism, flirtatiousness*

This card indicates you're totally wrapped
up in romantic ideas. Because knights signify messengers and travel, this card can
mean you receive a message—perhaps
an expression of love—from a suitor. If
this Knight represents an actual person,
he's probably a young man with a poetic,
imaginative, and affectionate nature, but
he might not be dependable.

### *Upright*

When this Knight appears upright, he can indicate changes and/or
travel—perhaps a vacation with a lover. Usually the change is a pleasant
one. It can also mean receiving an offer or invitation that sounds exciting, but it may not be practical or even doable. If the Knight of Cups represents a real person, he's someone who's fun but immature, unsure of
his true feelings, and likely to bolt at the first sign of difficulty. You may
be fascinated with him but probably shouldn't take him too seriously.

- In a reading about money, the Knight can represent a bold venture
but not a practical one. He may indicate carelessness with money and
possessions. He can also show a change in your finances, which could
be good or bad, or receiving word about a financial matter.

*The Modern Witchcraft Book of Tarot*

- If the reading is about your job, the upright Knight suggests you'll have a chance to use your imagination and creativity. Sometimes it shows travel, a job change, or relocation for work. It can also advise you to get serious and commit yourself if you want to succeed.
- In a reading about love, this card represents an exciting romance but not one that's likely to last long. Enjoy yourself, but try not to lose your head. The upright Knight may also signify a relationship with an artistic person.

*"The KNIGHT OF CUPS . . . is the KNIGHT of the grail legend. The story of the grail search is an allegory of seeking truth, beauty, purpose, and salvation in life."*

—SUSAN LEVITT, INTRODUCTION TO TAROT

### The Knight on a White Horse

Some decks, including the Rider-Waite-Smith and the Thoth Tarot, show the Knight of Cups riding a white horse, a romantic depiction of love—the fairy tale knight on a white charger come to carry you away to a fantasyland.

## Reversed

When the Knight of Cups appears reversed, he may represent insecurity, indecision, lack of commitment, and immaturity, especially in relationships. Sometimes he represents broken promises or deceit, or an offer that's not based in reality. If he stands for an actual person, he's someone to avoid. He's not what he seems—he may not even know himself who he is. Even if his intensions are good, he can't fulfill them.

- In a reading about money, this card warns, "Get out while you can." Someone may be trying to swindle you, or an investment isn't sound. A financial adviser may be untrustworthy or an offer is too good to be true.
- If the reading is about your job, the reversed Knight can show dishonesty, deviousness, or incompetence—either on your part or that of an employer or colleague. A project may not get off the ground. If you're considering a job change, this card advises against it.

- In a reading about love, the Knight reversed indicates secrets and lies in a relationship. A partner isn't being open or is conflicted about his or her feelings. Commitment isn't an option. This card may also say you're living in a fantasy world—stop dreaming and get real.

# PAGE OF CUPS

*Keywords: Naivety, openness, sensitivity, immaturity, lack of boundaries*

In some tarot decks, the page appears as a child, an apprentice, a student, or a young servant. Consequently, page cards represent innocence or the initial stages of a situation. Sometimes the Page of Cups is shown contemplating a fish, a symbol of the water element. When the Page of Cups shows up, it suggests intuition and innate artistic/creative abilities, but you haven't developed these yet. It also indicates emotional immaturity. If this card represents an actual person, he or she is probably young, inexperienced in love, and perhaps overly trusting, naive, or idealistic in the extreme.

## *Upright*

When the Page of Cups appears, it can indicate self-esteem issues. Perhaps you look to others to define you or place too much trust in people. It also suggests a keen intuition and latent artistic ability. Sometimes this card shows you facing an emotional issue about which you feel uncertain or unprepared. It can also represent the early stages of a relationship. If the Page stands for a real person, he or she may be a younger sibling, child, or friend, particularly an imaginative, sensitive, or idealistic one.

- In a reading about money, the Page indicates naivety in money matters. Perhaps you've got your head in the clouds or don't know how to

*The Modern Witchcraft Book of Tarot*

manage your finances. Sometimes this card recommends seeking guidance from an expert, but it can also show you're too trusting of others.

- If the reading is about your job, this card may represent the beginning of a new job or creative venture. Or, it can mean you're studying to improve your skills and marketability. Sometimes it urges you to stand up for yourself, instead of trusting others in your workplace.
- In a reading about love, the upright Page may signify the first blush of a romance. It can also mean you feel shy, vulnerable, or uncertain about a relationship. Perhaps you tend to give too much of yourself and trust too much—you'd benefit from a more equitable situation.

## Reversed

The Page of Cups reversed often indicates pain resulting from an unhappy relationship or family situation. As a result, you feel insecure, afraid to trust, unwilling to seek love because you want to avoid more suffering. This card can show fear of rejection if you express your creative abilities or reveal your intuitive nature. Sometimes it means you're withdrawing into a fantasy world. The reversed Page can also represent a sensitive young person who feels unaccepted or unloved or who can't trust anyone.

- In a reading about money, the reversed Page advises against relying on others for financial advice. Or, it may indicate a venture you're considering isn't well founded. Sometimes this card means you're underpaid or being taken advantage of and need to stand up for yourself.
- If the reading is about your job, this card may indicate disappointments, broken promises, or a situation that didn't turn out the way you'd hoped. It can also show misplaced trust—maybe you've been duped or betrayed in a work-related area. Or, you may not be using your talents wisely.
- In a reading about love, the Page reversed warns you to take a good, hard look at a relationship. This card may show you repeating a pattern of heartbreak and betrayal rooted in childhood. Perhaps you've opened your heart to the wrong person or fantasized that a romantic fling is something more serious.

# ACE OF CUPS

*Keywords: New love, beginning a creative activity, joy*

A single large chalice appears on the Ace of Cups. Sometimes water flows out of it, fountain-like, or the cup sits in water. In the Rider-Waite-Smith deck, a hand emerging from a cloud offers the cup as a gift to you. This represents a gift of love, either of a personal or divine nature. This Ace reminds us of the Holy Grail, the most famous chalice of all, which some people believe now lies in the Chalice Well in Glastonbury, England.

---

### A Wiccan Blessing

Sharing a beverage in a chalice is a popular practice in Wiccan rituals. Sometimes the chalice is offered with the blessing, "May you never thirst." Because the chalice is passed from one person to another, it may feature a long stem that makes it easier to handle.

---

## Upright

The upright Ace denotes a burst of joy, the kind that comes with falling in love. Often its appearance heralds a new romance, but it can also represent the start of a creative project about which you feel happy. When this beautiful card shows up, it indicates you're on an emotional high and enjoying life. Sometimes it indicates the birth of a child or idea.

- In a reading about money, the Ace suggests the beginning of a creative endeavor that promises to be profitable. Nurture it carefully and the seeds will bear fruit.
- If the reading is about your work, you may be starting a new job and feel enthusiastic about it. Perhaps this position will allow you to express your creativity or fulfill a dream, even though it might take some time.

*The Modern Witchcraft Book of Tarot*

- In a reading about love, the Ace symbolizes the first stages of a romantic relationship. Nurture it, so your love will blossom. Sometimes it represents awakening to divine love.

### Reversed

The reversed Ace can indicate a delay in starting a relationship. It can also mean a romance that seemed promising doesn't develop or turn out as you'd hoped. This may not be the right time to start something new.

- In a reading about money, the reversed Ace suggests you may have to wait a while to profit from a new venture. Or, it can mean you won't make as much as you'd expected.
- If the reading is about your work, you may encounter delays in landing your dream job. For creative people, this Ace can represent a "dry" spell when you feel stifled or uninspired.
- In a reading about love, you may run into obstacles, limitations, or disappointments.

## TWO OF CUPS

*Keywords: Partnership, harmony, creative exchange, cooperation*

In many decks, the Two of Cups shows a man and woman holding chalices as if toasting each other. The card represents joining forces with someone, either romantically or in a creative/spiritual endeavor. You share a common dream, interest, or passion and can work together to bring it into being. Mutual respect and equality exist between you.

### Upright

The upright Two indicates a period of harmony, when things go smoothly between you and another person. I think of this as the "honeymoon card," when you have high hopes and experience a time of accord, optimism, inspiration, and goodwill.

- In a reading about money, the upright Two suggests a financial partnership or merging your resources with someone else's for mutual gain. It can also mean financial support comes from a partner or backer.
- If the reading is about your job, this card describes a partnership that benefits both people. You inspire one another and enjoy working together. It can also represent cooperation and creative collaboration in your workplace.
- In a reading about love, the Two upright symbolizes a happy relationship that's developing smoothly. You understand each other's needs and bring out the best in one another. This card shows harmony, balance, and mutual respect between two parties.

### Origins of the Toast

According to the *International Handbook on Alcohol and Culture*, raising glasses in a toast recalls the ancient tradition of offering sacred libations to the goddesses and gods in hopes of receiving favors from them. The Greek god Dionysus and his Roman counterpart, Bacchus, are perhaps the best-known wine-drinking deities, but mythology also raises its glass to the Zulu fertility goddess Mbaba Mwana Waresa; the Sumerian beer goddess Ninkasi; the African "party girl" goddess Yasigi; and Sucellus, the Celtic god of alcoholic drinks.

### Reversed

When the Two of Cups appears reversed, it suggests disharmony and a lack of cooperation. It may mean a partnership takes a while to get going or that you run into obstacles. In some cases, it indicates dwindling affection, inequality, or a lack of supportiveness in a relationship.

- In a reading about money, the reversed Two can signify an uneven investment of resources. It can also represent complications or a delay in receiving money, especially from a joint venture, trust, divorce settlement, or legacy.

*The Modern Witchcraft Book of Tarot*

- If the reading is about your job, this card may mean you don't feel a business partner is pulling his or her weight or you don't get the support you desire. It can also point to a lack of cooperation in your workplace.
- In a reading about love, the reversed Two sometimes represents a secret liaison. Or, it may point to a period of disharmony or cooling affection. Perhaps there's a lack of balance or equality in a relationship.

# THREE OF CUPS

*Keywords: Celebration, fulfillment, friendship, community, happiness, fun*

The Three of Cups in many decks depicts three young women holding chalices aloft as if toasting each other. In some packs, the women are dancing and clearly having fun. A positive card, it suggests you have something to celebrate, perhaps a relationship or the success of a project.

### Upright

The upright Three says you're enjoying a good time with people you care about and admire. You could think of this as the "cheers card." It can also indicate expressing love, inspiration, and creativity with a community of like-minded people. The common bond between you "fills your cups" and brings blessings to all.

- In a reading about money, the Three says you can profit from a collective undertaking. It shows you reaping rewards from an investment made with other people.
- If the reading is about your job, the upright Three assures good fortune from a group effort. You feel joyful and fulfilled with the results. It's time to celebrate your success.

- In a reading about love, this card can represent a marriage. It shows you celebrating your love and extending affection beyond your primary partnership to include friends, community, and kindred spirits.

---

### The Three Graces

Greek mythology speaks of three goddesses of joy, charm, and beauty known as the Graces. The Three of Cups reminds us of the famous painting *Primavera* by the Renaissance Italian painter Sandro Botticelli, which shows these three beautiful young deities dancing together.

---

## Reversed

When reversed, the Three of Cups can indicate indulgence in food or drink—too much partying. Perhaps you feel weary from too much interaction with other people and need some downtime, or you've become disenchanted with your friends. In some cases, it shows a longing for friendship or sense of community.

- In a reading about money, rewards from a group effort may be delayed or not as great as you'd hoped. This card can also warn of overextending yourself financially or "counting your chickens before they're hatched."
- If the reading is about your job, the reversed Three suggests your success comes in small ways rather than grand ones. Or, a victory may seem hollow. Perhaps you don't feel as happy with your job or the results of a project as you'd expected to be.
- In a reading about love, the Three reversed shows you may feel left out, discouraged, or lonely. Perhaps you've grown and your lover/loved ones haven't kept up. In some cases, this card can mean a primary partnership takes up all your time and you don't get to see friends as much as you'd like.

# FOUR OF CUPS

*Keywords: Withdrawal, rest, boredom, lack of inspiration*

The Four of Cups in the Rider-Waite-Smith and other decks depicts a lone person sitting beneath a tree; some show a disembodied hand passing him or her a cup. The idea is that you've gone off on your own and aren't receiving what others hold out to you at this time. You may be withdrawing from your usual routine, work, friends, etc., in order to get in touch with yourself.

## Upright

The upright Four of Cups symbolizes boredom and stagnation. You're not satisfied with your life at this time but lack the incentive to make changes. You've detached emotionally from people and situations. Sometimes this card indicates you've sacrificed happiness for security.

- In a reading about money, this card can mean you're too attached to money and security, perhaps at the expense of love and joy. Perhaps you've prioritized money in the past and now seek meaning in other things.
- If the reading is about your job, you probably feel stuck and bored with your job. You may long for more creativity and enjoyment but have opted for security instead.
- In a reading about love, the Four shows you withdrawing affection and energy from a relationship. Perhaps routine has sapped your enthusiasm. This card also symbolizes a relationship based on security rather than passion.

## Reversed

The Four of Cups reversed is actually more positive than the upright Four. It indicates you need some time and space for yourself. Maybe you've been engaged in lots of activity lately and could really use a breather. Or, an intense emotional situation has left you feeling worn out and you just want to be alone to regroup.

- In a reading about money, this card recommends evaluating your ideas about money and possessions. Sometimes it suggests freeing yourself from expenses that drain your energy and keep you trapped.
- If the reading is about your job, you realize it's time for a change and may be seeking within for guidance. The reversed Four can also indicate exploring a spiritual path that will bring more meaning to your material existence.
- In a reading about love, this card says you may be reassessing a relationship that's lost its luster. The reversed Four can warn against rushing into a new affair indiscriminately. If you've recently ended a relationship, take time to be alone for a while before getting romantically involved again.

# FIVE OF CUPS

*Keywords: Disappointments, sadness, loss, loneliness, heartbreak*

One of the saddest cards in the tarot, the Five of Cups often shows a solitary person standing among overturned chalices spilling their contents onto the ground. The sense of despair, hopelessness, and grief is painful to see. Although five is the number of change and movement, this card suggests an inability to rise above a sadness, loss, or disappointment and move on.

## Upright

A setback has left you feeling helpless and hopeless, and you can't see a way out of your pain. Most likely, you've brought the loss or disappointment on yourself. The Five of Cups shows you're focusing on what

*The Modern Witchcraft Book of Tarot*

you lack rather than what you have—or could have if you changed your attitude. I think of this as the "self-pity card."

- In a reading about money, this card says you've endured losses—but all isn't lost. Don't keep throwing good money after bad. The Five also encourages you not to give up hope. In some cases, it warns against a financial matter you're considering.
- If the reading is about your work, you feel unvalued, unfulfilled, and unhappy in your current position. Find a job you'll enjoy more.
- In a reading about love, the upright Five can signify the end of a relationship. You feel hurt, disappointed, perhaps resentful. This split may open new possibilities for you.

---

### There May Be Opportunities

The Rider-Waite-Smith and many other decks show three cups overturned and two upright. This suggests all is not lost to the person for whom the reading is being done. Opportunities exist, but the querent may be so enmeshed in sadness and self-pity that she or he can't—or won't—see the possibilities that would lead to a happier place.

---

### Reversed

The Five of Cups reversed is less painful than the upright Five. It suggests you're not yet certain how to handle a disappointment or loss, but you're starting to move away from the hurt and make a new life for yourself. A card of healing, it represents acknowledging the struggles that make us stronger.

- In a reading about money, the reversed Five shows you've endured losses but are doing your best to recover. Just because you've undergone a setback doesn't mean you won't gain in the future.
- If the reading is about your job, this card advises letting go of anger and sadness about a disappointment. Things didn't pan out the way you'd hoped, but bemoaning the situation is a waste of energy. What you've learned from this experience can help you in the future.
- In a reading about love, you have to let bygones be bygones. Remember the old saying, "When one door closes, another opens."

# SIX OF CUPS

*Keywords: Nostalgia, emotional renewal,*
*happiness, harmony*

This joyful card sometimes shows two children in a garden—it represents reflecting on a time of innocence, contentment, and beauty. When it shows up, it indicates you're revisiting pleasant memories and good times. Knowing that you have been happy in the past can enhance your ability to be happy in the future—especially if you've undergone a painful experience recently.

## *Upright*

A card of emotional renewal, perhaps after a time of unhappiness, the Six of Cups represents a willingness to share joy with others. You eagerly give of yourself and receive the good things life offers. Through your actions, you express love and caring to people you know and to the things you value.

- In a reading about money, this card suggests an upswing in your finances, perhaps after a loss or time of limitation. It can represent a joint venture in which you share expenses and profits with others. Sometimes it indicates a debt repaid.
- If the reading is about your job, the Six upright shows renewed enthusiasm for your work. Perhaps a change offers you more creativity or an improved work environment. Developing new skills can benefit you now.
- In a reading about love, this card shows you're overcoming problems in a relationship and renewing positive feelings for one another. Sometimes the Six of Cups can mean reconnecting with a past lover.

*The Modern Witchcraft Book of Tarot*

*Reversed*

Because the Six of Cups is such a happy card, it signifies pleasant things even when it's reversed. It can show you strengthening your emotional muscles, building on past successes that will aid you in the future. However, it may mean you're stuck reminiscing about the "good old days" and can't seem to find happiness in the present.

- In a reading about money, you may be clinging to a time in the past when your financial picture was brighter. By refusing to look at new options, you may be limiting yourself.
- If the reading is about your job, you may be releasing old responsibilities in order to move forward. However, you may long for times when your career offered more excitement. Sometimes this card represents retirement.
- In a reading about love, the reversed Six can mean it's time to grow up and leave childish romantic fantasies behind. In some cases, this card shows you deepening your feelings and taking a more mature approach to a relationship.

### Symbol of a Kiss

The Six of Cups in the Rider-Waite-Smith deck shows a large cup resting on a pillar decorated with an "X." X is the Norse rune for love and a symbol we use for a kiss.

# SEVEN OF CUPS

*Keywords: Possibilities, potential, imagination, fantasy*

In some decks, including the Rider-Waite-Smith and the Aquarian, the Seven of Cups shows seven chalices holding a variety of objects—some pleasant, some frightening—which are being offered to the person who receives this card. When the Seven of Cups appears, it represents a time of contemplating options, weighing possibilities, and entertaining fantasies about your future.

### Upright
The upright Seven suggests many choices and paths are available to you now, but you may have trouble deciding among them. Nothing is certain. Let your intuition as well as your intellect guide you.

- In a reading about money, financial issues are colored by idealism. You have lots of ideas for making money, some inspired, some pure fantasy. Be careful with money and investments now—you're probably not seeing things clearly.
- If the reading is about your job, you seek a creative occupation and may be considering various options. However, you may not be realistic about your abilities or the possibilities open to you. Examine your choices carefully, especially if something seems too good to be true.
- In a reading about love, you feel romantic and may enjoy a highly emotional relationship with a person who inspires you. If you're not in a relationship, the Seven suggests you're contemplating what you really want, maybe indulging your fantasies.

### Reversed
The reversed Seven can mean either you're in a fog about your future or, conversely, you're finally gaining clarity about your direction in life.

*The Modern Witchcraft Book of Tarot*

Perhaps dreams you held in the past no longer interest you and you're replacing them with new goals.

> *"In the shamanic realm, this is about dispelling illusions to see the reality within, and about facing the worldly temptations that cause . . . the downfall of so many gurus and leaders."*
> —MARY K. GREER, *THE COMPLETE BOOK OF TAROT REVERSALS*

- In a reading about money, deception is a possibility—someone else may be unreliable or you may be deceiving yourself.
- If the reading is about your job, your ideas and projects may not bear fruit, partly because you lack the incentive and focus to move them along. Perhaps you feel lazy or uninspired—you'd rather dream than work.
- In a reading about love, the reversed Seven can indicate lack of commitment or indecision in a romantic affair. You want to keep your options open indefinitely. Or, you may idealize a relationship all out of proportion, refusing to see the truth.

# EIGHT OF CUPS

*Keywords: Turning away, cutting losses, decline, dejection, seriousness*

This card often pictures a person with his or her back to us, walking away. Sometimes a waning moon overhead symbolizes decrease. When the Eight of Cups appears, a situation has become untenable and you have decided to turn your back on it. Now you must strike out in another direction.

### Upright

You wish things had turned out differently, but you can't salvage a matter, and you realize you must abandon it. It's time to let go and get out of the situation that has failed despite your best efforts. Move ahead with determination—find a new direction and learn from your experience.

- In a reading about money, an investment hasn't paid off or you've lost money through no fault of your own, except, perhaps, not seeing things accurately. Cut your losses and conserve your resources.
- If the reading is about your job, the Eight of Cups may recommend pouring your heart and soul into an endeavor. Don't let distractions throw you off course. Sometimes this card advises leaving a job that no longer interests you.
- In a reading about love, this card can mean ending a relationship that's lost its spark. Conversely, it may show you getting serious about a partnership, giving it your all. You're no longer interested in casual flings.

*"When you most feel like holding on to something, it is usually the best time to let go."*
—DAVID CAMERON GIKANDI, *A HAPPY POCKET FULL OF MONEY*

### Reversed

The reversed Eight can mean you choose to stick it out and devote yourself to making a situation work—and sometimes it does. You could get a second chance and succeed eventually. Other times this card shows you wandering aimlessly, uncertain about your path, unable to commit to a relationship, longing for escape.

- In a reading about money, this card may recommend redoubling your efforts—in the end things will probably turn out satisfactorily. However, it can indicate you're confused or overwhelmed about financial matters and don't know how to get things in hand.
- If the reading is about your work, you may be unwilling to leave a job that's not right for you or is going nowhere. Is inertia keeping you stuck in a rut?
- In a reading about love, the reversed Eight can mean you're holding on to a failed relationship because you fear being alone. Sometimes, however, this card may indicate working on a troubled relationship, perhaps with the help of therapy.

# NINE OF CUPS

*Keywords: Wishes come true, good luck, happiness, abundance, generosity*

Often called the "wish card," the Nine of Cups is one of the most fortunate of all cards and bodes well in any reading. Some decks show a wealthy person, perhaps a tavern owner or innkeeper, sharing his or her largess with others— "filling their cups."

## Upright

You've achieved a position of comfort, abundance, and happiness. Now you eagerly share your warmth, love, good cheer, and other goodies with people you care about. The universe is smiling on you.

- In a reading about money, you can expect good fortune when this card appears. An investment pays off, you get a raise, maybe even win the lottery. Rather than hoarding your loot, however, you share some with others.
- If the reading is about your job, the Nine of Cups suggests a promotion or landing the job of your dreams. You feel fulfilled, happy, and inspired in your work. Whatever you undertake brings success.
- In a reading about love, you've learned to open your heart and enjoy a richly rewarding love life. This card may describe a joyful, emotionally fulfilling, committed relationship or an abundance of romantic partners.

*"Nature is held together by the energy of love."*
—Deepak Chopra, *The Seven Spiritual Laws of Success*

## Reversed

Reversed, the Nine of Cups can indicate indulgence, excess, and/or smugness about your riches. This card may also mean your errors are revealed, especially if your gains were ill gotten. In some cases, it shows you turning away from the material world to follow a spiritual path.

- In a reading about money, the reversed Nine may show you're spending more than you make or that you're pouring too much money into a venture. Or, it may reveal errors in judgment related to a financial matter.
- If the reading is about your job, this card may mean you're playing when you should be working. Perhaps you think you can rest on your laurels, but that's a mistake. Sometimes it suggests you've gained through questionable means or by allying yourself with unscrupulous people.
- In a reading about love, the Nine reversed can indicate frivolousness, promiscuity, or insensitivity in relationships. In some cases, it warns an indiscretion may come to light.

# TEN OF CUPS

*Keywords: Comfort, happiness, domestic bliss, love, harmony*

A card of fulfillment, the Ten of Cups represents a happy home where love and harmony abide. Some decks show a contented couple gazing at their beautiful home, while their children play. Others picture the pair with flowers, rainbows, and other symbols of love and hope. You could think of this as the "happy ever after card."

### Upright

Like other tens, this card signifies a time of completion, when you reap the rewards of what you've sown. Life is good. Abundance—in the true sense of the word—is yours.

- In a reading about money, you're in a position of financial security and comfort. Your efforts pay off. Sometimes this Ten represents family money, an inheritance, or marrying into wealth.
- If the reading is about your job, the upright Ten heralds rewards, respect, and recognition. You're proud of what you've accomplished and content with your success. This card can also mean working in a successful family business.
- In a reading about love, this card represents a loving, supportive, joyful relationship. It indicates a happy family life, where the people involved share love openly and feel secure in their situation.

## Reversed

The reversed Ten may point to disharmony or disappointments in your home life—things haven't turned out the way you expected. Sometimes it suggests a family that puts too much emphasis on "stuff" and not enough on love. In some cases, this card may represent the loss of a home or children leaving home.

- In a reading about money, the Ten reversed can mean having to scale down your expenditures and lifestyle. Sometimes it shows declining property values or squabbles over an inheritance.
- If the reading is about your job, this card says you're not as secure as you'd like to be. Problems within a company may threaten your position. Or, a company may grow too fast or overextend itself, requiring you to work extra hard.
- In a reading about love, a partner may not share your values or may have different ideas about family life. Maybe you don't get along with the in-laws, or kids from a former relationship cause problems.

# Chapter 8

# THE SUIT OF PENTACLES

Take a few minutes to look at the cards in the suit of pentacles. In early tarot decks, pentacles were associated with the merchant class and tradesmen. Therefore, storytelling decks often show people on the pentacle cards engaged in some type of monetary endeavor or physical labor: buying and selling goods, plying a trade, or building something substantial. For example, the Three of Pentacles in some decks shows an artisan working on a cathedral; the Eight pictures a craftsman at his workbench.

---

### The Inverted Pentagram

People who don't understand witchcraft, magick, or the tarot sometimes mistakenly associate the inverted pentagram with Satanism. Nothing could be further from the truth. Because the upright pentagram symbolizes the human body, the upside-down pentagram standing precariously on its point signifies imbalance—heels over head. It also indicates placing material things above spiritual ones.

---

Sometimes called coins, discs, pentagrams, or stars, pentacles are linked with money, material possessions and resources, practical matters, security, and the physical world. In a reading, these cards describe your finances, your ideas about money, how you earn your livelihood, how you handle money, what resources you possess, and how you interact in the mundane world. They may also refer to the physical. A representation of the feminine force in the universe and linked with the earth element, pentagrams in witchcraft are symbols of protection.

# KING OF PENTACLES

*Keywords: Security, material success, pragmatism, stability, strength, worldly power*

In many decks, this King sits on a throne and wears rich garments and a crown. Sometimes he appears with a bull, symbol of strength, virility, and tenacity. In a reading, he may represent an actual person, in which case he's usually a mature man who exercises worldly power and authority.

### Upright

When the King of Pentacles appears upright, he signifies a practical matter, finances, property, career/work, common sense, and security. If he represents a real person, it's someone who's a pillar of the community, a business leader, a person of wealth and substance, perhaps your boss or father. You can depend on him for support or advice in practical areas.

- In a reading about money, this card shows you're in a secure position financially. An investment should pay off, or you're advised to go ahead with a money matter you're considering. Good organization and practicality will benefit you.
- If the reading is about your job, the King shows success coming to you. Your position is stable, and you're using your resources wisely. You can take the lead in a business venture.
- In a reading about love, this card indicates a mature, stable relationship in which you support one another. Sometimes it shows a relationship based on money, status, or security.

### Reversed

When reversed, the King of Pentacles indicates sluggishness, delays, and/or obstacles to material success. Sometimes it shows low energy or insecurity. You feel stuck but don't have the drive to get out of your rut.

If the card represents an actual person, he may be mercenary, coarse, dull-witted, or even corrupt.

- In a reading about money, your finances are stagnant—you might even incur losses, perhaps because you're stuck in old patterns and have resisted making changes. You're worried about money and/or don't handle your resources well.
- If the reading is about your job, the King reversed may mean you're bored with your work but can't find something better. Perhaps you've sacrificed your passion for security. Or, your job may be in jeopardy and you feel insecure.
- In a reading about love, a relationship may offer stability but little excitement or romance. Routine or responsibility may drain your vitality. Perhaps you feel stuck in a relationship for financial reasons.

# QUEEN OF PENTACLES

*Keywords: Comfort, security, wealth, generosity, managerial ability, fertility*

Like the King, the Queen of Pentacles often appears seated on a throne, wearing rich garments and a crown. Some decks show her gazing down at a pentacle in her lap, symbolizing fertility. This card may represent an actual person, usually a mature woman who's intelligent, serious, and strong.

### Upright

The upright Queen suggests financial savvy and a keen understanding of the material world. When she appears, she indicates success in an area involving money or other resources. An undertaking should bear fruit if nurtured carefully. This is a "harvest card." If the Queen represents an actual person, she's a practical, wise, generous individual with a sensual side—she's at home in her body and enjoys her creature comforts.

## Earth Mother

We often refer to our planet as Mother Earth, and witches consider the earth to be feminine. In the Rider-Waite-Smith deck, the Queen of Pentacles sits in a beautiful landscape, which indicates her strong connection with nature. She's the ultimate earth mother.

- In a reading about money, the upright Queen suggests using money and resources creatively and constructively. She can also indicate a financial partnership or sharing resources with others.
- If the reading is about your job, this card can represent teamwork or a work-related partnership. It may show you bringing your creativity into a business matter. You nurture your own talents and help others develop their skills.
- In a reading about love, the Queen suggests a mature, sincere relationship. You enjoy sensual and sexual pleasure, creature comforts, financial security, and the good things in life.

### Reversed

When reversed, the Queen of Pentacles may indicate a questionable financial situation. Sometimes it shows a lack of understanding in money matters, mismanaging property, reckless spending, or hoarding. Envy or manipulation may exist when this card appears reversed. It can also suggest indulgence and laziness, or it may represent caretaker burnout.

- In a reading about money, the reversed Queen says you're not dealing with money matters in a constructive, realistic way. An investment or business venture may be shady or won't pay off. Your finances may be unstable or an adviser/partner may not be reliable.
- If the reading is about work, you may feel insecure in your job/ status and engage in questionable behavior to hold on to your position. Sometimes this card can indicate you've sold your soul for security and feel trapped and unfulfilled as a result.
- In a reading about love, the reversed Queen suggests an unhappy relationship based on security, status, or wealth. In some cases, it represents sexual excess, obsession, or trading sex for financial benefits.

# KNIGHT OF PENTACLES

*Keywords: Steadfastness, practicality, caution, lethargy, narrowness, boredom*

KNIGHT of PENTACLES

Many decks depict the Knight of Pentacles astride a horse, dressed in armor. Often he rides a dark horse, because dark colors symbolize stability, groundedness, and connection with the earth. The horse may stand at "parade rest," all four feet on the ground, to emphasize these qualities. Because knights represent communication and travel, this one may refer to a message about money or a trip for business/financial reasons. If he signifies an actual person, he's probably a young man with a practical nature who feels a strong connection with the physical world.

## Upright

If this Knight represents a real-life person, he's not a flashy or adventurous or even a particularly creative guy, but you can depend on him, and he's willing to do what's necessary to bring his goals to fruition. Money, possessions, and status mean a lot to him. He often succeeds through determination and effort, not inspiration or genius. Symbolically, this card speaks of perseverance, dedication, loyalty, and steadiness in the face of change or turmoil.

*"You have fought some battles and enjoyed some adventures. Now you'd like to rest and regroup, maybe spend some time enjoying quieter, more domestic scenes."*

—Barbara Moore, *The Gilded Tarot Companion*

- In a reading about money, you may receive information about money matters or an investment. This card can also indicate profiting from a practical investment or endeavor or selling property. Be content with slow gains rather than sudden windfalls.

*The Modern Witchcraft Book of Tarot*

- If the reading is about your job, the upright Knight can mean changing jobs for a more financially lucrative position or traveling for business. Sometimes he represents a career in finance or one connected with farming, real estate, construction, or manufacturing.
- In a reading about love, this Knight indicates stability, practicality, and loyalty. He may not be the most romantic or inspired lover, but you can rely on him. This card can also point to a relationship based on security, financial or otherwise.

### Reversed

Reversed, the Knight of Pentacles can mean stagnation, stubbornness, an inability to step outside the box, and traditional ways of doing things. Lack of imagination or courage can limit success. If the reversed Knight signifies an actual person, he's probably a young man without vision or curiosity—a "stick-in-the-mud." He may lack spiritual insight because his focus is on money and material possessions. Sometimes the reversed Knight shows a hedonistic nature or a willingness to take the low road if it leads to wealth or status.

- In a reading about money, this card suggests you're so caught up in making money you can't enjoy anything else. Conversely, it may say you lack the patience, persistence, and pragmatism to prosper.
- If the reading is about your job, the reversed Knight indicates boredom—but you aren't willing to do what's necessary to improve your lot. Laziness, lack of direction, indulgence, or feelings of unworthiness can inhibit your success.
- In a reading about love, you're bored but unwilling to put in the necessary effort to revive a romance; you're just slogging along. Perhaps a relationship is based on security, financial or otherwise. You long for a change, but you're afraid to go for it.

# PAGE OF PENTACLES

*Keywords: Study, developing resources, naiveté, curiosity, potential, service*

Pages often represent the early stages of a matter or a time of study and gaining skills. Some tarot packs picture the Page of Pentacles as a young person gazing at a pentacle, as if trying to understand it. If this card represents an actual person, it's probably someone young, intelligent, hardworking, and ambitious.

## *Upright*

The Page of Pentacles can point to the everyday details of your life and advise you to take care of them. This may refer to your work, possessions, or health. In some cases, this card may indicate naiveté in financial or practical areas—you're learning how to live in the real world. The Page can also show you performing a service for someone.

- In a reading about money, this card may refer to contracts or other paperwork related to money, possessions, or property. The Page upright may describe the early stages of a project, when you're discussing possibilities, seeking financial support, or laying the groundwork. You're advised to learn all you can about a money matter.
- If the reading is about your job, you may be preparing yourself for a career or a career change. A position in business, healthcare, or the trades could be profitable. The Page advises you to work hard and learn all you can, in order to reach your goal.
- In a reading about love, you may be more concerned with security, stability, and the practical aspects of a relationship than with romance. This card can also indicate meeting a partner through work.

## *Reversed*

When the Page of Pentacles appears reversed, it can mean you're not taking your training, work, or responsibilities seriously enough. Perhaps

*The Modern Witchcraft Book of Tarot*

you're bored, lazy, or just not up to the task. Lack of focus or follow-through could cause disappointments. In some cases, the reversed Page indicates you're out of touch with practical issues. Health-wise, it can suggest low vitality or depression.

> *"What one does is what counts and not what one had the intention of doing."*
>
> —PABLO PICASSO

- In a reading about money, this card may mean you're undercapitalized or ill-equipped to handle a financial matter. Perhaps you're too idealistic and haven't fully examined the practical aspects of a venture. Or, you may emphasize wealth, to the exclusion of other things.
- If the reading is about your job, the reversed Page may show you're reluctant to take a job you feel is beneath you. Or, you might be unprepared for the tasks facing you. Sometimes this card means turning away from the material world to pursue a spiritual path.
- In a reading about love, you may seek a partner who provides financial security or takes care of you—the "purse or the nurse" syndrome. Or, it may mean you're not holding up your end of a relationship's responsibilities.

# ACE OF PENTACLES

*Keywords: A financial start, opportunity, focus, ambition*

Many tarot decks depict this card as a big, bright pentagram that signifies potential abundance. In the Rider-Waite-Smith deck, a hand coming out of a cloud holds the pentacle in its palm, suggesting an offer is being extended to you. Indeed, the Ace of Pentacles represents the beginning of a project, venture, undertaking, investment, or other action in the material world. It's a card of opportunity—the other cards in the spread will show what you're likely to do with it.

---

### Nature's Bounty

In the Rider-Waite-Smith deck, a lovely garden blossoms with flowers on this card, showing its connection with nature's abundance. A hedge with an arched doorway gives a glimpse of mountains in the distance, which symbolizes the Ace of Pentacles's potential for material success in the future.

---

## *Upright*

This card symbolizes the start of a new business, financial venture, or other practical endeavor. It represents "sowing seeds," putting forth the initial effort—monetary, physical, and otherwise—needed to achieve the success you desire. Opportunities come your way now. Be pragmatic, realistic, and willing to work hard to bring your dream to fruition.

- In a reading about money, the Ace represents a new investment or financial endeavor. Perhaps you'll soon receive info about a money-making opportunity. Plant seeds carefully and, with effort, they'll bear fruit.
- If the reading is about your work, this card suggests you may be starting a new job that will profit you. You may be required to work

hard to bring a project, business, or career to fruition, but this card says success is likely.

- In a reading about love, the upright Ace says you may meet a partner through work-related avenues. It can also suggest launching a business/financial endeavor with a partner. Sometimes this card recommends taking a practical approach to a relationship.

## Reversed

The reversed Ace suggests you're overly concerned about money and possessions. It may indicate greed or hoarding, or an attachment to material goodies causes you to miss out on other things in life.

- In a reading about money, this card can refer to stagnant finances or missed opportunities. You may experience delays in getting money you're due, or you may not receive as much as you'd expected.
- If the reading is about your job, you may feel stuck in a rut, perhaps in a job that pays well but isn't stimulating. You're bored but unwilling to take a chance on something new. Sometimes it means doors aren't open to you at present.
- In a reading about love, the reversed Ace can describe a relationship based on money and/or security, rather than true love. A partnership may seem restricting or may limit your options. Sometimes it suggests a missed opportunity for love.

# TWO OF PENTACLES

*Keywords: Balance, busyness, financial partnership, choices, ups and downs*

Some decks picture a person juggling two pentacles, which represents juggling different facets of your life. You're trying to keep many balls in the air, so to speak. Sometimes this card indicates making a choice between two things.

## *Upright*

The upright Two can mean good fortune as a result of your ability to handle many things at once. You manage to balance work and play and feel content with your situation. Sometimes it shows you have many resources at your disposal and know how to use them well.

- In a reading about money, the upright Two may mean doubling your money. Perhaps by joining forces with a partner, you can profit more than you could alone. In some cases, this card indicates two sources of income.
- If the reading is about your job, the Two can represent balancing work with downtime—you need both to stay happy and healthy. It can also indicate a busy period when you have to juggle projects or duties. Sometimes it suggests choosing between two job offers or opportunities.
- In a reading about love, this card may represent shared resources or working with a romantic partner, perhaps running a business together. It can also mean you're trying to balance your work and domestic life. Sometimes it indicates a choice between two partners.

## *Reversed*

When the Two of Pentacles appears reversed, it may mean you have your hands full and feel overwhelmed. You're having trouble balancing work and leisure time. It can indicate instability in financial matters, uncertainty in your work situation, or concerns about a health issue.

- In a reading about money, you may go through a period of ups and downs financially. Money comes and goes quickly, and you have to juggle your resources to stay afloat.
- If the reading is about your job, the reversed Two can indicate working two jobs to make ends meet. Changes in your workplace may cause you to feel anxious about your position.
- In a reading about love, this card can mean you feel restless in a relationship. Financial concerns may cause problems in your personal life. Perhaps one of you is shouldering a bigger share of responsibilities and you need to establish better balance.

*"Always choose love over safety if you can tell the difference."*
—Josephine Humphreys, *Dreams of Sleep*

# THREE OF PENTACLES

*Keywords: Creativity, self-expression, skill, satisfaction, rewards*

The card of the craftsperson, the Three of Pentacles often depicts a skilled artisan at work. In some decks, he's building a cathedral, reminiscent of the carpenters and masons who constructed Europe's great cathedrals and who evolved into the Freemasons. Threes signify self-expression, creative development, and reaping rewards, so this positive card shows a time of satisfaction.

## Upright

The upright Three represents expressing your creativity in a practical way and enjoying your work. You've developed your skills; now you gain rewards and recognition from applying your talents constructively. Other people too derive pleasure from what you do. This card can also encourage you to market a product, idea, or talent.

- In a reading about money, this card indicates profiting from your work. You could think of it as the "payback card" when your efforts bear fruit. It may also show a financial endeavor coming to fruition or at least beginning to prosper.
- If the reading is about your job, you're using your abilities fully and achieving success. What you create now should have lasting results you can be proud of and enjoy. The upright Three may signify the satisfactory completion of a project or job.
- In a reading about love, you've worked through challenges and invested a lot of effort in a relationship. Now things are on the upswing and you can enjoy your relationship. Contentment and security are yours.

## Reversed

When the Three appears reversed, it can mean you're not making the best of your abilities. Perhaps you lack confidence or can't find a way to use your talents. This card may advise developing new skills to compete in a rapidly changing marketplace.

- In a reading about money, the reversed Three can mean money for a project doesn't come through or cost overruns plague you. Perhaps you don't receive as much as you wanted for your work or property or must accept a cut in pay.
- If the reading is about your job, you may not get the recognition or rewards you deserve for your efforts. Plans may not work out, delays may occur, or problems with coworkers/clients may interfere with your success.
- In a reading about love, this card may indicate you feel unappreciated by a partner. Perhaps you've invested a lot in a relationship, but your efforts aren't paying off, or your partner doesn't reciprocate as you think he or she should.

# FOUR OF PENTACLES

*Keywords: Security, materialism, caution, possessiveness, greed, creative blocks*

In some tarot decks, the Four of Pentacles features a man with four pentagrams attached to his body. The image suggests his money and possessions define him. Fours symbolize stability; therefore, this card signifies financial security—or seeking it.

## Upright

The upright Four represents a practical, conservative attitude toward money and material goods. You place great value on wealth and possessions and take pride in your worth. Because security is important to you, you hold on tight to what you own and may hoard money rather than enjoying it. You could think of this as the "miser card."

- In a reading about money, this card can indicate a cautious, prudent attitude toward financial matters. You play it safe and devote yourself to accumulating wealth. The upright Four may signify a sound investment or a stable financial position.
- If the reading is about your work, you've chosen a job that's secure and provides a good income, perhaps one in finance. Wealth gives you status and power, which you value. However, you may not feel inspired, challenged, or content in your position.
- In a reading about love, the upright Four represents a stable, secure, structured relationship. The partnership may be based on status and money rather than love and may lack passion.

## Reversed

When the Four of Pentacles appears reversed, it suggests your conservative attitude and limited vision are causes of stagnation. As a result, you encounter obstacles and delays that keep you from moving ahead.

You need to make changes, to stop clinging to old ideas and tried-and-true methods, but you're afraid to take a risk.

- In a reading about money, this card recommends against an investment or financial venture at this time. Sometimes it indicates imprudent spending or bad decisions regarding money or property.
- If the reading is about your job, the reversed Four can mean you feel insecure in your position. Outsourcing, cutbacks, or competition may threaten your job. You may be passed over for promotion or fail because your skills are outdated or inadequate.
- In a reading about love, you may fear losing control in a relationship. Because you sense your power dwindling, you feel insecure. Perhaps you depend on your partner for financial support and feel trapped in the relationship.

---

### Greed

You've heard the saying, "Money is the root of all evil," but the actual quote is, "Love of money [greed] is the root of all kinds of evil." In some tarot decks, this card is labeled "Greed." The Thoth Tarot, however, calls it "Power" and gives a more positive interpretation—a solid foundation on which you can create something sound.

---

# FIVE OF PENTACLES

*Keywords: Poverty, disappointment, loss, lack, restriction, disorder, worry*

Often this card depicts a couple or a family in an attitude of humility, poverty, or hardship. Their desperation and suffering are evident. Sometimes a stained-glass church window appears above them, which indicates emphasizing spiritual values over material ones.

### Upright

I think of this as the "need card." You're in a pinch and need help—don't be too proud to ask for it. Usually the Five of Pentacles represents financial need, although it may point to a health issue or a disappointment in another physical area. Sometimes it suggests you're not using your resources wisely—you may not even be aware of your potential.

- In a reading about money, the Five points to losses, financial woes, debt, and feelings of desperation. However, it can also indicate paring down your lifestyle and assessing what's really important. Perhaps spiritual things mean more to you than material ones.
- If the reading is about your job, you may feel financially strapped because you're not earning enough to pay the bills. Work-related responsibilities may drain your vitality. Maybe it's time to look for a better job.
- In a reading about love, the Five of Pentacles can mean a relationship is draining your energy—you're investing a lot and not getting much in return. This card suggests emotional poverty, limitations, and unhappiness.

### Reversed

When the Five of Pentacles appears reversed, it can indicate recovery—or persistence—after a period of adversity. You reach deep down into your inner reserves to find the strength to carry on. Sometimes the card says the worst is over. It can also mean turning away from the material world to follow a spiritual path.

- In a reading about money, the reversed Five can show you've hit rock bottom and the only way is up. A card of renewed fortune, it signifies digging your way out of a hole and recovering—financially or health-wise—perhaps with the help of others.
- If the reading is about your work, it can mean losing a job but finding something you like better, even if it doesn't pay as much. Sometimes this Five represents freedom from responsibilities. Or, it can indicate regrouping after a time of loss or disorder.
- In a reading about love, the reversed Five may suggest letting go of an unfulfilling relationship and seeking something better. Or, it can show you emerging from a difficult time and doing what's necessary to repair the damage.

# SIX OF PENTACLES

*Keywords: Give and take, generosity, prosperity, good fortune, cooperation*

This card represents generosity and sharing resources with others. It also points to a time of financial security and balance. Some decks picture a man of means holding a scale on which he can weigh gold (or other goodies). The Six of Pentacles represents a time of good fortune, when you can afford to be charitable.

## Upright

The upright Six heralds good times ahead, particularly in financial/material areas. You can profit from cooperative ventures, combining your talents and sharing resources for the greater good. This card can also represent philanthropic projects or providing work for other people. You could think of this as the "win-win card."

- In a reading about money, the upright Six can signify an opportunity to participate in a group venture that will profit everyone. Sometimes it points to acquiring a loan or other financial backing.
- If the reading is about your job, the Six represents teamwork. You may participate in a group effort that uses your talents; combining your abilities or resources with others' promises success.
- In a reading about love, the upright Six suggests sharing resources— financial and otherwise—with a partner so you both benefit. This give-and-take card encourages you to open up to what a partner offers, and vice versa.

*"Be content with what you have;*
*rejoice in the way things are.*
*When you realize there is nothing lacking,*
*the whole world belongs to you."*

—Lao Tzu

## Reversed

Reversed, the Six of Pentacles can show unfair financial dealings, unreliable colleagues, or unpaid debts. Perhaps a project or investment doesn't materialize as you'd hoped or the strings attached to it choke you. Sometimes the reversed Six suggests relying on others for financial support, even taking advantage of their goodwill.

- In a reading about money, the reversed Six may mean getting involved in a questionable financial endeavor that compromises or obligates you in some way. The payoff may not be what you expected, or you feel unsatisfied with the way your money is handled.
- If the reading is about your job, you may have difficulty balancing your needs and aspirations with those of your employer. You may become disillusioned at how a company handles resources and responsibilities.
- In a reading about love, you may feel an inequity in the balance of power. Perhaps your needs aren't being met, or you aren't meeting your partner's needs. The reversed Six recommends focusing on give and take in a relationship, supporting and encouraging each other.

# SEVEN OF PENTACLES

*Keywords: Growth, accomplishment, commerce, appraisal*

Some tarot decks show a person examining a tree or bush on which seven pentacles hang, like ripe fruit. Thus, the Seven of Pentacles represents watching the seeds you planted mature. An investment of time, energy, and/or money is starting to pay off, and you're assessing the result.

## Upright

The upright Seven shows a venture or financial investment beginning to bear fruit. However, you may still need to put in more work and be patient—you haven't reached the end yet. As you appraise your "crop," you may choose to prune the tree, discarding the lesser-quality fruit to improve your harvest.

- In a reading about money, you're starting to see gains, but there's still room for growth. Don't give up. The Seven also warns against get-rich-quick schemes. Use prudence.
- If the reading is about your job, the upright Seven shows you advancing in your career and advises you to continue applying effort. What you do now will impact future results.
- In a reading about love, you may feel a relationship is taking too long to warm up or that you're not making much progress. However, the upright Seven encourages you to continue taking small steps—little by little things are improving.

### The Magickal Septagram

To witches—especially those who follow a faery tradition—the septagram, or seven-pointed star, is a magick and sacred symbol. Sometimes it's called a faery star or elven star.

*The Modern Witchcraft Book of Tarot*

### Reversed

The reversed Seven often signifies anxiety, impatience, and concerns about losses. You doubt you'll reach your goal, or worry that the outcome won't live up to your expectations. Sometimes this card indicates procrastination or lack of enthusiasm needed to complete a project.

- In a reading about money, the reversed Seven warns of losses or setbacks. Even though you've put in a lot of effort, you don't net the profits you feel you deserve. Sometimes this card represents working too hard for what you earn.
- If the reading is about your job, you may not get the recognition or rewards you'd expected. Perhaps you fear someone is trying to undermine you. Obstacles and delays may occur, or a project may not turn out as well as you'd hoped.
- In a reading about love, this card can show distrust, suspicion, or fears about a relationship's stability or a partner's loyalty. Whether or not it's true, you feel insecure and worry that a partner's affection is dwindling.

# EIGHT OF PENTACLES

*Keywords: Craftsmanship, skill, work, sincerity, determination, integrity, focus*

Like the Three of Pentacles, the Eight represents skilled effort, and many decks show a craftsman plying his trade on this card. You have an important goal in sight, and you're willing to work hard to achieve it.

### Upright

The upright Eight heralds success in an endeavor. You've honed your skills to a high level, and you're totally focused on your purpose. Because you pursue your objective with sincerity, clarity, and determination, your efforts reap rewards.

- In a reading about money, this card can represent receiving a raise, landing a well-paying job, or profiting from a venture. Do what's necessary to reach your financial goal.
- If the reading is about your job, the upright Eight says your craftsmanship will be rewarded with recognition and respect. You're immersing yourself in your work in order to get ahead; with continued effort you'll succeed. Sometimes this card means you can benefit from gaining additional skills.
- In a reading about love, you realize a relationship takes work, and you're willing to put forth the necessary effort. You and your partner take a mature attitude toward your relationship and are dedicated to each other. Sometimes this card represents love coming late in life.

---

## Midlife Crisis

Anna Franklin, in *The Sacred Circle Tarot*, links this card with a midlife crisis and sees it as particularly beneficial for artists who, in maturity, devote themselves to their work.

---

### Reversed

The reversed Eight shows you working hard but not getting ahead. Maybe you feel like a hamster in a treadmill, running as fast as you can but going nowhere. You could think of this as the "burnout card." Delays, obstacles, or confusion may interfere with your success. This card can mean you lack the necessary skills to accomplish your aims.

- In a reading about money, this card can signify bills piling up or maxing out your credit cards. Perhaps you simply don't earn enough to make ends meet. It may also represent depending on someone else for support, rather than earning your own way.
- If the reading is about your job, you may hold unrealistic ideas about your abilities; therefore, you're disappointed when you don't get the job, promotion, or respect you seek. Perhaps laziness, substandard skills, or lack of focus is to blame.
- In a reading about love, the reversed Eight can suggest work or money problems may be wearing you down and interfering with your relationship. It can also show boredom, insincerity, or waning affection.

*The Modern Witchcraft Book of Tarot*

# NINE OF PENTACLES

*Keywords: Abundance, material well-being, security, comfort, success*

Some decks, including the Aquarian and the Rider-Waite-Smith tarot, depict a woman with a beautiful bird, standing in a vineyard. The ripe fruit symbolizes a period of plenty and accomplishment— it's time to harvest your crop.

## Upright

Nines represent fulfillment, and this lovely card says you've arrived. You've achieved your goals and now feel secure. You've worked hard, used your skills and acumen, and accomplished much—you have reason to be proud. The upright Nine also represents independence—you've created the life you desire and can now enjoy your success.

---

### A Self-Made Woman

Some tarotists, including Barbara Moore, author of *The Gilded Tarot Companion*, see this card as representing the self-made woman, independent of a man's support and rightful proprietor of her own domain. Only twenty-seven years before English-born Pamela Colman Smith began her series of paintings that would become the Rider-Waite-Smith tarot deck, England's Parliament passed the Married Women's Property Act of 1882, which allowed married women to own property. Before that time, a woman surrendered her holdings to her husband upon marriage, and any property she gained during the marriage became her husband's.

---

- In a reading about money, this card indicates you have plenty and no longer need to worry about financial security. Enjoy the fruits of your labors—you've earned them. The vineyard can also suggest acquiring property or earning a nice profit from selling property.
- If the reading is about your job, the upright Nine indicates a time of success and recognition. You've reached a position of security and

respect, and feel proud of your achievement. Perhaps you now have more independence or free time; sometimes this card can signify retirement.

- In a reading about love, this card shows a secure, comfortable, pleasant relationship—or, conversely, it says you're content to be alone and don't need a partner. This Nine may symbolize a relationship that offers financial abundance and ease without limiting your freedom.

### Reversed

The Nine of Pentacles reversed may mean you depend on someone else financially. Although your situation may be comfortable in the material sense, you feel trapped or bored. You'd like to get away, spread your wings, but responsibilities hold you back. Perhaps you don't feel satisfied with your success or don't feel you deserve it.

- In a reading about money, the reversed Nine may indicate squandering money or losing property, perhaps due to theft, damage, or deception. If you're purchasing or selling property, this card recommends caution.
- If the reading is about your job, this card can signify boredom or a lack of freedom in your work. Perhaps you feel you should've accomplished more or achieved a higher position by now. You may long for a vacation (or retirement) but can't afford to leave your job.
- In a reading about love, you may feel stifled or disenchanted in a relationship. The reversed Nine can symbolize a partnership, based on money and/or security, that lacks excitement or romance. It can also suggest lack of independence or equality—one person holds the reins.

# TEN OF PENTACLES

*Keywords: Abundance, fulfillment, inheritance, good fortune, property, family resources*

The last of the pip cards in this suit, the Ten represents fulfillment and abundance. In some decks, the Ten of Pentacles shows a happy couple, perhaps with a child, observing their luxurious home contentedly. The card has connections with family—especially family money and property—but also the legacy of inherited resources such as good health, intelligence, cultural benefits, etc. You have plenty and can now share your riches with others.

## *Upright*

The upright Ten promises pleasure, abundance, and security in your professional and domestic life. You enjoy your work and your family, and your income allows you to provide for loved ones. Comfortable in your financial position, you can now devote yourself to leisure activities or perhaps philanthropic ventures.

- In a reading about money, the upright Ten points to prosperity and stability in money matters. Sometimes it represents family money, an inheritance, or marrying into money. It can also mean profiting from an investment, particularly one involving property.
- If the reading is about your job, this card may mean working in a family business. Your job provides security, wealth, and worldly success, and you enjoy what you do. Perhaps you work in real estate, farming, or another property-related occupation. In some cases, the upright Ten represents a philanthropic venture or business that helps others.
- In a reading about love, this Ten indicates a happy, successful, secure family life. Maybe you now feel financially stable enough or mature enough to start a family. Or, you may marry into a wealthy family.

## Reversed

You may be so established at this point that you're stagnating. Maybe you've retired comfortably and now just sit around watching TV. The reversed Ten of Pentacles can indicate problems with family members, perhaps frustration, disagreements, or responsibilities regarding a family business, property, or inheritance.

- In a reading about money, the reversed Ten can represent losses or debt, which may be related to family troubles or obligations. Or, it can mean you don't inherit as much as you'd expected. Family feuds over money/property are possible. This card can also point to fluctuations in the marketplace or real estate values that threaten your security.
- If the reading is about your job, you may not be using your resources and abilities fully, or you may not receive the compensation and success you feel you deserve. A business—perhaps a family operation—may hit hard times. Sometimes this card shows you rejecting the material world for the spiritual one.
- In a reading about love, financial and/or family problems may cause friction and unhappiness in a relationship. Responsibilities for children or elderly parents might place strain on you. Emotional baggage and old hurts may interfere with your happiness.

# Chapter 9

# THE SUIT OF SWORDS

Take a few minutes to peruse the cards in the suit of swords. In early tarot packs, this suit represented the knighthood and the aristocracy, which ruled by the power of the sword. Therefore, some storytelling decks show knights or nobles on the cards. Today we associate this suit with states of mind and mental activity, communication, the world of ideas, psychological matters, and spiritual issues.

You'll notice the cards frequently depict challenging situations, hardship, or sorrow. The suffering associated with the swords may result from overanalyzing situations or from cutting yourself off from your inner self. Although some writers, particularly in older texts, put a negative spin on these cards, many contemporary tarotists pay attention to the swords' spiritual aspect too. Indeed, we sometimes come to a spiritual path as a result of intense suffering, be it physical, mental, psychological, or emotional.

Like wands, swords are phallic symbols that represent the masculine force in the universe. They're linked with the element of air, the witch's athame (ritual dagger), and the suit of spades in a regular playing deck. Some decks refer to them as daggers, knives, sabers, arrows, or other terms.

---

## Life Is Pain

An old Chinese proverb says, "Life is pain. Pain makes you think. Thinking makes you wise. And wisdom makes life endurable." The swords represent this perspective.

---

# KING OF SWORDS

*Keywords: Judgment, intelligence, mental power, communication*

In some decks, the King of Swords sits on a throne, wearing royal robes and a crown and brandishing a mighty battle sword. Other decks show him in military armor. In a reading, he may represent an actual person, in which case he's usually a mature man known for his intelligence, communication skills, fairness, and objectivity.

KING of SWORDS.

## *Upright*

The upright King represents intellectual pursuits, communication, spiritual knowledge, and study. You may be mastering a mental task or using your communication skills successfully. Sometimes this card indicates a decision, judgment, or legal matter. If the King signifies an actual person, he may seem stern, analytical, or aloof—perhaps he's a lawyer or judge, a professor, military leader, scientist, or religious leader.

- In a reading about money, the King upright recommends taking charge of a financial matter. Do your homework—don't let your emotions influence a decision involving money or investments. This card may also mean profiting from an intellectual endeavor.
- If the reading is about your job, it may indicate you work in a field that requires keen intelligence, good communication, or analytical ability. The King advises you to show leadership regarding decisions or judgments—clarity and objectivity are important.
- In a reading about love, the King symbolizes a relationship based on shared interests and ideas rather than passion. You and/or your partner resist expressing deep emotions, preferring a friendly partnership. Perhaps you fear losing independence if you open your heart.

*The Modern Witchcraft Book of Tarot*

## Reversed

When the King appears reversed, he can indicate mean-spiritedness, biting wit, arrogance, judgmental attitudes, or narrow-mindedness. If he represents an actual person, he may be someone who lacks compassion and can even behave cruelly, perhaps a harsh religious leader or an unscrupulous lawyer. Or, he may be fickle, indecisive, absent-minded, or gossipy. I think of this as the "watch your back card."

- In a reading about money, the reversed King warns that losses may result due to unprincipled people, a business that's not on the up and up, or a legal matter. Poor judgment can cause problems too. Clarity and honesty are needed now—pay attention to details.
- If the reading is about your job, you may feel your boss is too harsh, your work too demanding, your colleagues too mean. Perhaps you think you've been treated unfairly. In some cases, this card may represent an organization or situation that's corrupt or at least shady.
- In a reading about love, the reversed King shows coldness, insensitivity, or dishonesty. You or your partner may be too critical, judgmental, or hurtful toward one another. Narrow-mindedness or arrogance may lead to nasty arguments.

*"I think the highest purpose of ritual or magickal work is to seek our gods, to commune with the cosmic 'mirror' and the spirits of nature in order to learn more of the divinity within ourselves and reach evermore toward personal growth in its highest expression."*

—Maria Kay Simms, *A Time for Magick*

# QUEEN OF SWORDS

*Keywords: Intelligence, independence, authority, objectivity, communication*

The Queen of Swords is the female counterpart of the King, except she represents the creative side of the mental process—the novelist rather than the accountant. In some decks, she sits on a throne, wearing a crown and a luxurious robe, holding a sword. The Aquarian Tarot pictures her crowned but *sans* throne, wielding her sword as a woman warrior, sort of a Joan of Arc or Athena figure. In a reading, she may represent an actual person, in which case she's usually a mature woman known for her intelligence, independence, and inner strength.

---

### Reach or Receive?

The Rider-Waite-Smith deck shows this Queen in profile, holding out her hand. Look at the other cards in a spread to see whether she beckons or turns away from you. Other cards in the spread may show what she reaches for or receives—also what she offers.

---

## *Upright*

The upright Queen of Swords represents authority, wisdom, and power. In a reading, she suggests you've gone through emotional trials and grown as a result. Your will is strong, and you possess the intellectual resources to take charge of situations, at home and/or in the business world. If she signifies an actual person, she may be a single woman, divorcée, or widow who's transformed pain into wisdom. Respected for her communication skills, she may be a writer, professor, lawyer, minister, business leader, or scholar.

- In a reading about money, the upright Queen recommends using social networks and joining forces with other like-minded people to profit—although the "profit" may go to a charitable cause she supports. Don't let your emotions influence financial decisions. Honesty is essential now, but don't reveal more than is necessary.

- If the reading is about your job, this card can indicate a career in a communication field. Your intelligence and objectivity can help you advance. Sometimes this Queen suggests you need to speak up for yourself, ask for what you want, and stand your ground.
- In a reading about love, you seek independence and equality in a relationship. Sometimes this card means choosing to remain single and/or childless in order to pursue intellectual or career goals. Shared ideas, ideals, and interests are more important to you in a partnership than passion.

### Reversed

When the Queen appears reversed, you may feel trapped, limited, unable to speak your own truth. She can indicate disappointments at work or home, broken promises, hopes that didn't manifest. You may feel you haven't been given a chance to show your stuff or you've been handed a puny piece of the pie. Perhaps you can't move beyond a loss or your emotions are interfering with your judgment.

- In a reading about money, this card can mean you've let your emotions rather than your intellect guide a financial matter. It may also suggest you've gotten bad advice or not investigated a situation adequately and consequently incurred losses. This Queen warns, "Read the fine print."
- If the reading is about your job, you may not be using your intellect and creativity fully. Or, you feel your abilities aren't appreciated. A boss may be too critical, coworkers may be envious or undependable, causing you to question yourself. The reversed Queen may represent the "glass ceiling" women still face.
- In a reading about love, this card suggests bitterness caused by disappointments or losses. As a result, you may swear off relationships and isolate yourself. Sometimes the Queen reversed shows an overly critical nature, inflexibility, or coolness toward a partner.

# KNIGHT OF SWORDS

*Keywords: Daring, chivalry, forthrightness, impatience, single-mindedness, insensitivity*

KNIGHT of SWORDS.

Knights often symbolize messages or travel; some decks, including the Rider-Waite-Smith tarot, show this Knight rushing hell-bent toward an adversary or adventure. In the Aquarian Tarot, however, he shoulders his sword, contemplating his next move. If he represents a person you know, he may be someone who's overly aggressive or argumentative, who lives in "attack mode." Or, he might be a spiritual warrior, one who uses his intellect to examine and purify himself.

## Upright

The upright Knight may suggest you're passionate about your ideas and believe wholeheartedly in the rightness of your objective. If this card represents an actual person, he's probably a young man who expresses his ideas enthusiastically and may have trouble understanding other viewpoints. He has a quick mind and keen intellect but may lack true wisdom. Sometimes this Knight symbolizes an urgent message or an unexpected trip.

### Knights and Athletes

Our modern-day athletic teams have their roots in the medieval period when knights served the royalty and noble houses. Our allegiance to particular teams—often connected to the schools we attended or the places where we live—recalls our ancestors' fidelity to the tribes, fiefdoms, or countries to which they belonged. Even the pennants waved at sporting events harken back to days of old, when soldiers carried banners into battle to indicate the side for which they fought.

- In a reading about money, you may need to act quickly in a financial matter—but don't neglect to study the situation before making a decision. The upright Knight may point to a trip for financial reasons or a message about money. Sometimes he heralds a change in your resources.
- If the reading is about your job, this card can represent a business trip. Sometimes it means a job change or a shift in work-related responsibilities. The Knight may also caution you to hold your tongue and bide your time—diplomacy is important now.
- In a reading about love, the Knight may point to a new affair or a change in an existing relationship that brings more freedom, excitement, and openness. It can also recommend being more flexible and tolerant.

### Reversed

The reversed Knight lacks the intensity, drive, and confidence of the upright Knight. When he appears in a reading, he suggests a lackadaisical attitude, indecision, confusion, or withholding information. If he represents an actual person, he may be a young man who doesn't say what he really means, who lives in his mind instead of the real world, or who's incapable of handling the tasks before him.

- In a reading about money, the reversed Knight may indicate imprudence in a financial venture. Either you haven't thought things through fully or you think you know everything. Losses may occur as a result. Don't act on impulse.
- If the reading is about your job, you may feel restless in your current position but haven't decided on a new course of action. Perhaps you're discouraged or angry about something in your workplace. Don't make waves or burn bridges—investigate your options dispassionately so you can make an informed change.
- In a reading about love, the reversed Knight suggests arguments, cutting words, or irresponsible behavior may cause a rift in a relationship. This card can also indicate dishonesty. Perhaps one of you wants more freedom and rebels against commitment and structure.

# PAGE OF SWORDS

*Keywords: Study, vigilance, apprehension, inexperience, curiosity, a message*

Pages represent study and apprentice-ship, and this card says learn to express yourself so you can communicate with sword-like precision. It might mean you're exploring new ideas or embark-ing on a spiritual quest. If the Page of Swords symbolizes an actual person, it's probably a clever and curious youth who hasn't yet mastered the power of his or her intellect. The Aquarian Tarot, for example, shows a boy with his sword at his side—he hasn't yet gained the confidence to wield it.

## *Upright*

When the Page appears upright, it may show you're thinking of branching out, testing yourself, embracing a challenge. Perhaps you're entering college, beginning a career, or starting off on a spiritual quest. Naturally you're anxious because you don't feel prepared. You may not have used your "sword" on the battlefield, but you've trained and devel-oped the skills you need to succeed. Trust yourself.

- In a reading about money, the Page can represent a message about a money matter. This card recommends examining details and inform-ing yourself, rather than simply relying on others for advice. How-ever, it also warns against overconfidence—ignorance can lead to losses.
- If the reading is about your job, this card shows you beginning a career that tests your intelligence and education. You may be start-ing a project that requires good communication skills. Or, you may be refining your mental abilities and clarifying ideas.
- In a reading about love, this card can indicate an immature or detached attitude toward relationships. Perhaps you're harboring an

unrealistic ideal about love. The Page may also suggest you're not ready to commit to a relationship—you have other things to do first.

## Reversed

Despite your intelligence, you may lack clarity or direction in life. When this card appears, it may indicate irresponsibility, idealism, impracticality, or frivolousness. Sometimes it suggests a narrow or rigid worldview that prevents new information from coming in. If the reversed Page represents a person you know, it could be a young, inexperienced individual or someone whose limited life experience and blinkered attitudes leave him or her at a disadvantage.

- In a reading about money, the reversed Page of Swords warns that lack of information or naiveté could lead to financial problems. Do you have your head in the clouds? Are you trusting advisers you shouldn't? Read the fine print and make sure you understand what you're getting into.
- If the reading is about your job, this card may represent disillusionment or confusion regarding your career path. Maybe you were enticed by promises that didn't materialize, or your dreams had no substance. Be careful about sharing information with colleagues/coworkers—they may not be trustworthy. The reversed Page can also mean you lack the skills needed to succeed.
- In a reading about love, you feel insecure or unequipped to handle the demands of a relationship. Perhaps you want time for yourself and aren't ready for a serious commitment. In some cases, this card can warn that a partner isn't what she or he seems or that indiscretion is afoot.

# ACE OF SWORDS

*Keywords: Focus, beginnings, new ideas, opportunity, truth, clarity*

Aces represent beginnings, and this card heralds the initial stage of a new idea, spiritual direction, course of study, or intellectual project. In the Aquarian Tarot, the sword is accompanied by two white roses, which symbolize love, spirituality, purity, and hope. In the Rider-Waite-Smith deck, a disembodied hand reaches from a cloud, holding out a crowned sword, suggesting you're being handed a message or opportunity from the divine realm.

---

### Cupid's Arrow

Instead of swords, the Lover's Path Tarot uses arrows for this suit and tips the arrow with a heart. According to author Kris Waldherr, the arrow belongs to Cupid and symbolizes "the power of love to create wisdom."

---

## Upright

This Ace indicates success through the use of mental means or spiritual growth. You're using your intellect in a clear, focused way, devoting yourself to a goal. An opportunity is being offered to you—grab it. Sometimes this card points to a breakthrough or inspiration.

- In a reading about money, the upright Ace represents the birth of an idea or start of an intellectual project that could bring profits. It can also mean negotiating a contract or discussing a financial issue.
- If the reading is about your work, this card suggests starting a job that involves communication. You have an opportunity to use your intellect productively or to express your philosophical/spiritual views in your work. Clarity and focus will help you get ahead. This Ace can also indicate starting a course of study that will further your career.

*The Modern Witchcraft Book of Tarot*

- In a reading about love, the Ace upright symbolizes a relationship in which you share ideas, inspire one another, and enjoy lively conversation. It can also mean a relationship with a mentally oriented person or one who can teach you much.

## Reversed

When the Ace appears reversed, it may warn that an idea isn't valid or that you're not yet clear in your own mind and shouldn't go ahead. Negotiations may break down or you may encounter delays with a project. Be sure to communicate clearly as misunderstandings can occur.

- In a reading about money, the reversed Ace indicates worries and stress regarding money. Perhaps someone isn't being honest or a contract has flaws. This card advises against an investment or large purchase at this time.
- If the reading is about your job, you may experience frustration or delays in getting an idea off the ground. Sometimes this card represents dishonesty, gossip, miscommunication, or arguments in your workplace.
- In a reading about love, the Ace reversed can represent coolness or detachment in a relationship. Perhaps you and a partner have trouble communicating or you argue a lot. Sometimes this card shows you hold different ideas or spiritual views.

*"The highest purpose of the Tarot is as a system of self-initiation or enlightenment. It is a map into the realms of spiritual bliss. It is a record of man's relationship with the cosmos. In short, it is a textbook of occult teachings."*

—GERALD AND BETTY SCHUELER, *THE ENOCHIAN TAROT*

# TWO OF SWORDS

*Keywords: Combined resources, courage, faith, friendship, conflict, balance*

In some tarot decks, this card depicts a blindfolded woman holding two swords crossed over her chest. Twos generally signify balance or conflict, as well as pairing. I think of the Two of Swords as the "blind faith card" because it can represent courage and making decisions based on your own truth—and in some cases, spiritual guidance.

## *Upright*

The upright Two can symbolize balancing the right and left hemispheres of your brain, combining intuition with intellect. Drawing this card may mean you must make a decision and need to call on both. This Two can also advise you to take off your blindfold and look at a situation honestly.

- In a reading about money, the upright Two recommends trusting your own wisdom and inner guidance in a financial matter. Pay attention to your intuition as well as logic.
- If the reading is about your job, you may be confused or conflicted about a work-related issue. Have faith in your own judgment and ideas. Sometimes the upright Two represents a job that requires both intellect and imagination.
- In a reading about love, this card suggests listening to both your head and your heart. It can mean you and your partner hold conflicting perspectives or that you're trying to resolve differences and find harmony.

## *Reversed*

Reversed, the Two of Swords often indicates confusion or conflict—with yourself or someone else. An imbalance may cause stress or frustration.

Sometimes this card urges you to take action, rather than endlessly analyzing a situation. You can't see ahead, but you must take a leap of faith.

- In a reading about money, this card suggests worrying about a financial matter. You don't know what to do and can't trust anyone to help you. The reversed Two can indicate choosing between two unsatisfactory options.
- If the reading is about your job, the reversed Two represents confusion, indecision, lack of information, or conflicts regarding your work. It can also warn that colleagues aren't reliable or trustworthy. You need to look hard at something you don't want to see.
- In a reading about love, confusion or differences of opinion may cause stagnation in a relationship. Are you clashing swords? Honesty and openness are important now. The reversed Two also represents imbalance—one person may wield more power than the other.

# THREE OF SWORDS

*Keywords: Suffering, heartache, regret, grieving, sorrow, loss*

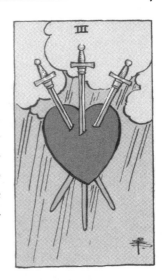

Just looking at this heart with three swords piercing it is painful. One of the saddest cards in the tarot, it symbolizes deep emotional pain, heartbreak, and a real or perceived tragedy. You may not manage to avoid the suffering indicated by the Three of Swords; however, the card advises separating true grief from self-pity.

## Upright
The upright Three signifies separation, severing a connection to something or someone you love. You feel isolated and cut off from something you found meaningful—a way of life, your home and family, a philosophy, pursuit, or job. Something in your life has died, usually because it has lost its meaning or run its course, and you need to let it go.

*"The soul . . . is . . . a diamond in the rough, which must abide the blows inflicted by suffering in order to shine in all its brilliance."*
—LAURA ESQUIVEL, *LIKE WATER FOR CHOCOLATE*

- In a reading about money, the upright Three represents losses due to relying on your rational mind or your emotions alone—you need to use both to avoid problems. Sometimes it suggests someone you trusted has withdrawn support or you're grieving the loss of better times.
- If the reading is about your work, this card can mean losing a job you loved. Or, you feel isolated and unhappy in your job. Maybe you regret an unwise business decision or you're thwarted, unable to do the work you enjoy. Try to see this as a sign: It's time for a change.
- In a reading about love, the upright Three can represent a split with a partner, or at least a sense of separation and despair. If the relationship is worth salvaging, heal the gap with compassion and understanding. In some cases, this card says it's time to move on.

### Reversed

The reversed Three of Swords is actually less problematic and severe than the upright Three. It suggests you're making more of an unhappy situation than necessary or that a disappointment is temporary—not the end of the world. Perhaps the truth hurts, but once you face it you can improve things. Pull yourself together and get on with your life.

- In a reading about money, you may harbor regrets about what might have been, or you're chastising yourself for a bad decision. The reversed Three recommends letting go of blame and guilt, repairing damage, and starting anew.
- If the reading is about your job, you may be pulling out of a damaging and hurtful situation. The reversed Three can mean the worst is over and you've learned from your mistakes. Remain watchful for confusion, deception, or poor judgment.
- In a reading about love, this card points to painful experiences, but you're working on past problems and trying to make things better. You need to let go of jealousy, regrets, guilt, and fear. Sometimes this card represents accepting a loss and moving on.

# FOUR OF SWORDS

*Keywords: Rest, recuperation, retreat, solitude, introspection, recovery*

Fours symbolize stability—this card represents withdrawing and resting in order to get your bearings after a time of trouble. Some decks show a knight lying down, recuperating after an inner or outer "battle."

## *Upright*

Often this card means you've been through a period of difficulty and now feel the need for introspection and solitude. You're examining what you've experienced, trying to understand what it all means, so you can plan for your future. This is the "calm after the storm card." Sometimes it shows you're starting to recover after a physical illness or injury.

- In a reading about money, the upright Four urges caution and discrimination. Maybe you need to separate yourself from a financial issue. This card can also suggest you feel overwhelmed by financial burdens and need a rest.
- If the reading is about your job, you probably feel burned out at work and need a vacation. After a period of stress, confusion, or difficulty, you may be sorting things out, clearing your head, and regaining your strength.
- In a reading about love, the Four upright can mean carving out some time for yourself. Challenges in a relationship may have left you feeling drained or discouraged. Look within to discover your true needs and how you can restore balance.

---

### Find Clarity from Doubt

In *Introduction to Tarot,* Susan Levitt writes, "Unfortunately, the mind is too often filled with worry, doubt, and fear. Or, the mind absorbs information that has little to do with the soul's inner workings." To counteract this, she recommends meditation, yoga, deep breathing, chanting, prayer, long walks, and baths.

---

## Reversed

The reversed Four indicates you need to rest but aren't giving yourself the time out you require. If you continue the way you're going, you could even make yourself sick. Unless you allow your mind, body, and spirit a chance to recover, the situation will grow worse.

- In a reading about money, the reversed Four can indicate remorse about a financial matter. Perhaps you continue pushing yourself to make money, depleting your energy, even though you really need to take a break.
- If the reading is about your job, you have trouble dealing with the stress and demands in your workplace but can't see a way out of the situation. Your head's spinning, and you're running on empty. Perhaps seeking advice from a counselor or someone you respect can give you a new perspective.
- In a reading about love, this card can signify giving up on a relationship—or giving in, with regrets. In some cases, it may mean a temporary separation so you can heal old wounds, gain clarity, and work on yourself.

# FIVE OF SWORDS

*Keywords: Change, adjustment, loss, destruction, conflict, indecision, sadness*

The number five signifies change, and this card shows a time of adjustment after a conflict of some kind. Sometimes the fight stems from ideological or spiritual differences. The Rider-Waite-Smith, Aquarian, and some other decks show a soldier on the battlefield at the end of a fight—the card asks, what have you won or lost?

## Upright

The Five of Swords symbolizes the devastation of war and recommends using diplomacy to resolve problems. After a "battle," you realize fighting isn't the best way to settle disputes. The cost of winning may not be worth the losses you've endured.

- In a reading about money, this card represents disputes over money, perhaps in a legal matter. It also warns that even if you "win" you may suffer. Try to resolve differences without "drawing swords." Vacillation or lack of clarity can cause setbacks too.
- If the reading is about your job, the upright Five cautions you to avoid arguments—don't make enemies. This card may also indicate you're confused about how to proceed or suggest you need to get more info before taking the next step.
- In a reading about love, this card says you won't get what you want by arguing. Hurtful words can't be taken back. Try to resolve problems amicably, honestly, and fairly. You may have to make some changes in order to improve a situation.

### Reversed

Reversed, the Five suggests pretty much the same thing as it does upright. When the card appears reversed in a reading, however, you may feel a great sense of remorse, regret, or unhappiness. Sometimes it shows you making repairs or reparations after a conflict, trying to set things right again and learning from your suffering.

- In a reading about money, the reversed Five can indicate losses after a fight, perhaps a legal matter or squabble over an inheritance. In the end, no one really wins and you may experience regret. Indecision or unwillingness to make necessary changes could be costly too.
- If the reading is about your job, struggles with bosses or coworkers may cause hard feelings or impede your progress. A conflict may damage your chances for advancement, perhaps causing you to change jobs under unfavorable circumstances.
- In a reading about love, this card can indicate mourning the loss of a relationship or regretting a decision made in the heat of an argument. Perhaps you feel betrayed. In some cases, however, it can suggest trying to repair the damage and make constructive changes, perhaps with the help of therapy.

# SIX OF SWORDS

*Keywords: Movement, escape, a change for the better*

The Six of Swords represents moving away from past troubles, putting them behind you. It marks the beginning of a new phase after a time of upheaval. Some decks depict a person in a boat, ferrying six swords—symbolizing pain, struggles, regrets, or losses—across a body of water so the wounds can heal on another shore.

## *Upright*

The upright Six suggests "smooth sailing" ahead, as you leave behind the trauma and sadness of the past. You're embarking on a new path, and the changes you make now are based in the wisdom you've gained through suffering. Sometimes this card symbolizes a journey, either of a physical or spiritual nature, perhaps a "vision quest."

- In a reading about money, you've learned much as a result of past difficulties and now have more clarity that can help you benefit financially. Sometimes this card recommends letting go of an investment or possession. It can also represent relocation or travel for financial reasons.
- If the reading is about your job, this card shows your work situation improving. Perhaps you've resolved past problems or you've chosen to move to a different position that suits you better. Sometimes the upright Six symbolizes a business trip.
- In a reading about love, the upright Six indicates you and a partner have resolved major problems and arrived at a place of harmony and understanding. Let bygones be bygones. In some cases, this card means leaving an unworkable relationship for something better.

## Reversed

The reversed Six can mean you're unwilling or unable to move away from a troubling situation. Perhaps you fear taking a leap of faith and leaving your old ways behind. Outdated attitudes may hold you back, however. Delays, obstacles, or other interferences—including input from other people—can also complicate your plans.

- In a reading about money, the reversed Six can mean you're leaving behind losses or a bad investment. In some cases, however, it suggests you're stuck in an old pattern or regretting a financial decision that didn't turn out well. Don't keep throwing good money after bad.
- If the reading is about your job, this card can indicate you're reluctant to move on after a painful experience. Perhaps you think you're at a dead end or doubt you can recover from a hardship, but this Six encourages you to marshal your energies and find a place where you can flourish.
- In a reading about love, the Six reversed warns against sticking with old, outworn beliefs and behaviors out of fear. Unhappiness results when you're unwilling to make changes that awaken your heart, mind, and spirit to new possibilities.

### Crossing Water

The ancient Chinese oracle known as the *I Ching* speaks of "crossing the great water," which means pushing ahead courageously, getting beyond a challenge, and growing as a result.

# SEVEN OF SWORDS

*Keywords: Uncertainty, illusion, impetuousness, stealth, cunning, strategy*

Some decks, including the Rider-Waite-Smith, Aquarian, and Gilded Tarot, show a man carrying away five swords, leaving two stuck in the ground behind him. When this card appears, it suggests you're facing a challenge or problem and must use caution to overcome potential danger.

## Upright

The upright Seven suggests a tricky situation in which things are not completely clear. You may be formulating a plan but don't have all the information you need. Or, the plan may be risky and could backfire. This card can represent surreptitious action and advises diplomacy.

- In a reading about money, the Seven warns that you probably shouldn't go ahead with a financial idea or investment you're considering. Perhaps the risks are too high. Or, the deal may be shaky or shady.
- If the reading is about your job, this card says don't engage in direct confrontation. Work behind the scenes to get results. The upright Seven can also indicate restlessness; perhaps your job lacks the diversity or stimulation you desire. Consider making a change.
- In a reading about love, you're advised to seek compromise and use diplomacy, rather than arguing with a partner—but don't just go along to get along. Sometimes this card shows leaving a relationship that doesn't meet your intellectual or spiritual needs.

### Focus

Be focused and thorough in planning your strategy. As Barbara Moore writes in *The Gilded Tarot Companion*, be on guard or "one of those swords he left behind will find its way into his back."

## Reversed

When the Seven appears reversed, it can mean either you're behaving impetuously or that you're overly cautious and afraid to act. It can also represent coming clean about a mistake and trying to make restitution. Sometimes this card shows you experimenting with different plans and getting various points of view.

- In a reading about money, be careful of get-rich-quick schemes, gambling, or dubious endeavors. The reversed Seven can represent deception or leaving yourself vulnerable. Sometimes it suggests you may have gained through (or are considering) underhanded means.
- If the reading is about your job, this card can warn of dishonesty or deception in your workplace. Perhaps you'll need to separate yourself from a situation—stay open-minded and flexible so that you can respond to changes quickly. It can also mean taking advantage of someone else.
- In a reading about love, the reversed Seven can mean apologizing for a mistake or injury. Perhaps you've betrayed, hurt, or manipulated someone. However, this card can also show you assisting a partner through a challenge or warning him or her against a risky course of action.

*"Tragedy should be utilized as a source of strength. No matter what sort of difficulties, how painful experience is, if we lose our hope, that's our real disaster."*

—His Holiness the Fourteenth Dalai Lama

# EIGHT OF SWORDS

*Keywords: Entrapment, self-undoing, fear,*
*helplessness, bondage, denial, deception*

In many decks, the Eight of Swords
shows a person bound and blindfolded,
ringed by a "prison" of swords. Because
swords represent thoughts and beliefs,
this card says you've created your own
prison with your ideas and only you can
free yourself.

### Upright

A card of self-undoing, this is the "you are
your own worst enemy card." You know you need to do something, but
you're unwilling to act. Perhaps you're in denial about a situation. Consequently, you're stuck in a painful state. However, the Eight upright
says you have the resources necessary to "get out of jail" if only you can
overcome your fear.

> *"Many of our fears are tissue-paper-thin, and a single courageous step*
> *would carry us clear through them."*
>
> —BRENDAN FRANCIS BEHAN, IRISH AUTHOR

- In a reading about money, you may feel your hands are tied, but that's
  an illusion. Still, you must make choices to free yourself from a limiting situation. Perhaps you've fallen into debt through unwise spending. Sometimes this card says be content with small gains.
- If the reading is about your job, fear of change or feelings of inad-
  equacy may be holding you back. As a result, you're blind to possibilities. Perhaps you're wasting energy or underusing your abilities.
  Upgrading your skills may help you advance.
- In a reading about love, this card suggests you feel trapped or unfulfilled in a relationship. However, you're contributing to the problem.
  Perhaps your expectations aren't realistic, or you need to change
  your attitude if you want to change the situation.

## Reversed

To break through the barrier you've built, you must change the way you see and do things. Sometimes this means rejecting social norms or going against the status quo. You also need to get focused and get moving. Perhaps you have your head in the clouds. The reversed Eight warns you to get your affairs in order or the situation could worsen.

- In a reading about money, this card says you may not be dealing forthrightly with a financial problem. If you've been putting off paying your taxes, for example, or settling a legal matter, take care of it promptly to avoid more trouble. Sometimes this Eight indicates bad advice or deception.
- If the reading is about your job, the reversed Eight tells you to stop playing the victim. You may feel persecuted, trapped, or limited in your work, but you must take responsibility for where you're at and do something about it.
- In a reading about love, you may feel tied to a person, perhaps because you're afraid to be alone or unwilling to support yourself. This card can mean you're not facing up to what's really going on. If you've been listening to someone else's advice, the time has come to listen to your inner guidance.

*"The only thing we have to fear is fear itself."*
—FRANKLIN D. ROOSEVELT, IN HIS FIRST INAUGURAL ADDRESS

# NINE OF SWORDS

*Keywords: Despair, isolation, sadness, fear, grief, shame*

The Nine of Swords shows extreme anxiety, nightmares, tension, unhappiness, regrets over past mistakes or misfortunes. In many decks, this card shows a person weeping while nine great swords loom above her or him. In the Rider-Waite-Smith deck, a woman sits up in bed as if waking from a nightmare. Because this suit represents mental activity, much of your suffering may be in your own mind.

*"Too many of us are not living our dreams because we are living our fears."*

—LES BROWN, MOTIVATIONAL SPEAKER AND AUTHOR

## Upright

You're agonizing about a problem, torturing yourself with worries and fears. This is the "dark night of the soul card," for it shows you reaching deep within yourself to deal with a crisis. However, you probably feel hopeless and helpless to handle the situation on your own. This card may refer to deep-rooted or repressed issues coming to the surface—perhaps in the form of nightmares—so you can resolve them.

- In a reading about money, this card represents anxiety, guilt, or desperation regarding a financial matter. Perhaps you're anguishing about a loss and kicking yourself for not having seen it coming. Sometimes the Nine advises downsizing. It can also mean money comes to you but at a high cost, such as an inheritance or insurance settlement.
- If the reading is about your job, you feel drained, unhappy, or fearful in your position. You may be faced with a crisis you can't handle,

or you're miserable in a job you don't think you can leave. Resisting only makes things harder. Sometimes this card signifies losing a job you love.

- In a reading about love, the upright Nine indicates suffering due to a hurt caused by someone you care about. You may feel rejected, unloved, lonely, or unvalued. This card can represent the end of a relationship or a desperate need to correct a problem in a relationship.

## Reversed

Nines signify completion, and the reversed Nine can point to the end of a crisis or a period of despair. You may have determined the root cause of your misery and are ready to deal with it. Perhaps you've stopped feeling sorry for yourself and are willing to make the changes necessary to repair the damage and move on. In some cases, this card may indicate getting professional help with a problem.

- In a reading about money, this card can mean you see where you made mistakes and begin the process of rebuilding after a loss. It may be difficult to pull yourself out of your doldrums, but the reversed Nine suggests the worst is over. Don't give up.
- If the reading is about your job, you may have suffered as a result of someone else's jealousy, criticism, or nastiness. However, this card encourages you to stand up for yourself and stop wallowing in fear or self-pity. It may also recommend changing jobs.
- In a reading about love, you may be examining a relationship deeply to decide if it's worth staying or if you'd be better off leaving. Sometimes being alone is preferable to remaining in an unhappy situation. Be honest—you may have deceived yourself for a while.

*"There are very few monsters who warrant the fear we have of them."*
—ANDRÉ GIDE, AUTHOR

# TEN OF SWORDS

*Keywords: Exhaustion, giving up, betrayal, pain, sadness*

In many decks, the Ten of Swords depicts a man lying on the ground with ten swords stuck in his back. Ouch! Tens represent the end of a cycle and the start of a new one. Therefore, this card symbolizes an end to the suffering and sadness you've endured. Just in time, for you probably couldn't stand much more.

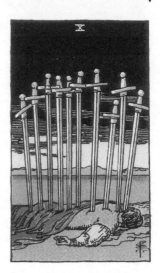

## *Upright*

Your trials and tribulations are ending, but you still need to clear away the deadwood before you can move ahead. Extreme stress and worrying have exhausted you—perhaps leading to an illness—but the storm has passed and the clouds will open up again. Make a clean break from the past to alleviate pain and suffering.

- In a reading about money, you may need to cut your losses, let go of possessions, and/or separate yourself from a past financial matter. Tie up loose ends, then move forward with the newfound insights you've gained from a painful situation.
- If the reading is about your job, this card suggests you're burned out mentally and perhaps physically. You've been under so much pressure you don't think you can go on. Fortunately, you've turned a corner and the road ahead looks brighter. Sometimes this Ten can represent backstabbing, so be on guard.
- In a reading about love, the upright Ten represents exhaustion after a period of hardship in a relationship. Sometimes it signifies betrayal. Or, it may represent the strain of caring for a loved one through an illness. Even if a relationship ends, you may look forward to starting over and being free from the troubles of the past.

*The Modern Witchcraft Book of Tarot*

## Reversed

Reversed, the Ten of Swords suggests you're unwilling to take the steps that will move you to a better place. Perhaps you're deceiving yourself or you're stalling due to fear, but delaying only makes things worse. Stop making excuses and choose a course of action.

- In a reading about money, the reversed Ten can represent a time of recovery after hardship or loss. A new cycle is beginning and better times may wait around the corner, but you must take the first step.
- If the reading is about your job, you still feel insecure about your future, but in order to get to a more satisfactory place you'll have to take a risk. Stop letting the past prevent you from embracing new possibilities.
- In a reading about love, you may still be smarting from a deception, disappointment, or betrayal, but at least you can see more clearly now. If a relationship has ended, you may experience a new sense of freedom.

*Chapter 10*

# THE MAJOR ARCANA

Now we come to the Major Arcana, the "soul" of the tarot. *Arcana*, as you know, means "secret," and the Major Arcana symbolizes life's great mysteries. The cards in this "book" represent higher, spiritual forces at work in our lives. Some people think of them as indicators of fate or destiny, karma or dharma at work. When a Major Arcana card shows up in a reading, it suggests spiritual forces beyond your conscious control are operating in the matter. You may even sense a higher presence, spirit guides, angels, or guardians with you as you read these cards.

> *"The beauty and richness of each card reflects clarity and wisdom. Each image and symbol has a message designed to empower us Spiritually and make every day and special life decisions easier."*
> —KISMA K. STEPANICH, *FAERY WICCA TAROT*

## THE FOOL'S JOURNEY

The Major Arcana is also known as the Journey of the Fool that leads from innocence to enlightenment. The Fool—the first of the Major Arcana or "trump" cards—symbolizes the emergence of consciousness, the first step on this magickal sojourn. The World—the last of the trumps—signifies the journey's end: union with the Divine. As a whole, the Major Arcana shows both the pilgrim's quest toward wisdom and the soul's trip back to the Source.

## Numerology and the Major Arcana

In the ancient study of numerology, twenty-two is considered a "master number" that resonates on the higher planes as well as the physical one. An extremely powerful number, twenty-two represents the master builder who can harness cosmic forces and use them to shape the material world. The number of transformation, twenty-two also serves as a bridge between the earthly realm and the spiritual one.

Each of the cards in the Major Arcana can be viewed as a lesson. Together, they describe all the possible experiences available to us during human existence. The individual lessons must be learned in order, and you must master a lesson before you can move on to the next. You can also think of the trump cards as chapters in a book—for the Major Arcana is a book—and you must read the chapters in order or they won't make sense.

## The Major Arcana and the Hebrew Alphabet

Some tarot researchers link the twenty-two cards in the Major Arcana with the twenty-two letters in the Hebrew alphabet. The Thoth Tarot, for example, makes this connection.

As you begin your study of the Major Arcana, think of yourself as The Fool. *Fool* is not a derogatory term—it refers to an innocent, child-like state in which you are open to receiving guidance and instruction. We often see The Fool depicted in myth and legend as the youthful hero who must go out into the world to seek his fortune. Along the way, he encounters numerous trials and adventures that build his character. In many stories, The Fool is the seemingly naive, bumbling sidekick who ultimately saves the day. The dunce wearing a pointed magician's hat is actually a magus in training.

> *"Now, it is the Arcana which stimulate us and at the same time guide us in the art of learning. In this sense, the Major Arcana of the Tarot are a complete, entire, invaluable school of meditation, study, and spiritual effort—a masterly school in the art of learning."*
> —ANONYMOUS, *MEDITATIONS ON THE TAROT*

# THE FOOL: 0

*Keywords: Innocence, beginnings, trust, hope, opportunity*

The first card in the Major Arcana, The Fool begins your journey toward wisdom. The Fool represents innocence and faith, the naive confidence of youth. Shown as a young traveler, he embarks on an adventure without a care in the world, unconcerned about the potential dangers that lurk ahead on the path. In some decks, he appears as a happy-go-lucky young male standing at the edge

of a cliff, just about to step off into the great unknown. Often he carries all his worldly possessions tied in a small bag on a stick over his shoulder, like a hobo, suggesting he doesn't have a lot of "baggage" yet and is open to life's experiences. In some decks, he's accompanied by a dog or another animal, which represents natural instincts. The Fool symbolizes the blind leap of faith we all must take upon entering the journey of life.

*"A journey of a thousand miles begins with a single step."*
—Lao Tzu

## Upright

When The Fool appears in a reading, it usually means you're about to embark on a new way of life. You're open to new experiences and to discovering what lies around the bend. Even if you're not sure about the path you've chosen, you have faith that everything will turn out well. You probably feel out of sync with the rest of the world, but in a good way. You hear the beat of a different drummer, and you're ready to march to it.

- In a reading about money, The Fool urges caution. You may be too trusting, or you may be naive when it comes to handling financial matters. This card can also represent the first stage of a business or investment—examine details carefully. Pay attention to your intuition, not only logic.

- If the reading is about your work, The Fool can indicate starting a new job, project, or business venture; beginning a course of study; or going on a business trip. You're looking forward to this adventure or new direction and its possibilities. Embrace the opportunity with an open mind—you have a lot to learn.
- In a reading about love, this card often means beginning a romance or moving into a new stage in an existing partnership. A new relationship may feel "fated," as if you've met your soulmate. Enjoy this period of joy, openness, and excitement.

> *"The quest for meaning always takes us into the unknown."*
> —F. ASTER BARNWELL, *THE PILGRIM'S COMPANION*

### Reversed

If The Fool is reversed, you may feel restless and bored, eager to try something new, but now's probably not the right time to act. I think of this as the "don't quit your day job card." That's not to say what you want is wrong-headed, but you need consider the pros and cons carefully before you walk off that cliff.

- In a reading about money, you may not have all the information you need to make a well-founded decision. An impulsive action could lead to a fall. Someone may take advantage of your innocence. The reversed Fool can also mean you're vacillating or overly cautious about money matters.
- If the reading is about your job, your current situation has probably led to a dead end or you've grown bored with the career path you're on. It's time to strike out in a new direction. Don't do this hastily, however. Gather information and explore possibilities.
- In a reading about love, this card can warn you to look more closely at a partner or relationship—things may not be what you think. The reversed Fool may also indicate the end of a relationship and greater freedom as a result. Think before you act, however, for you might regret a breakup undertaken hastily.

# THE MAGICIAN: 1

*Keywords: Hidden power, magickal ability, mastering unseen forces, inner guidance*

A powerful and wise figure, The Magician represents the ability to understand and command the unseen forces that operate in the universe. Usually he's depicted as a male figure who stands alone with the tools of his trade before him—as a witch, you'll surely recognize them: the wand, chalice, pentagram, and athame. As discussed in Chapter 2, these tools also appear as the four suits  in the Minor Arcana. The Magician's knowledge enables him to manipulate the material world by aligning it with the spiritual plane so he can create the circumstances he desires. That's what you do when you cast spells—that's the essence of magick!

When The Magician shows up in a reading, he indicates you have special powers, but you may not realize them yet or you may not be using your powers. Use your intellect, intuition, talents, and practical skills to manifest your dreams. The Magician reminds you that you're constantly creating your reality and that your thoughts are the forerunners of manifestation. He can represent your inner guide who, if you listen carefully, will help you fulfill your potential.

*"Magic is believing in yourself. If you can do that, you make anything happen."*

—JOHANN WOLFGANG VON GOETHE

### Upright

The Magician recommends getting in touch with the unseen world instead of focusing only on the material one—they aren't separate, and what we usually think of as "reality" is an illusion. The presence of the four magick tools (which also represent the four elements, as discussed in Chapter 3) on this card suggests that everything you need is right there at your fingertips. You're connecting with your power and aligning yourself with universal forces to achieve your goals and desires.

- In a reading about money, The Magician tells you to tap into the universal flow to attract abundance. You possess the resources—inner and outer—to generate wealth. This card can also advise you to take control of a financial matter.
- If the reading is about your job, this card encourages you to use your spiritual and physical resources correctly to take command of your life and master the circumstances around you. Trust yourself and your inner guidance. The Magician can also symbolize a position in a spiritual field or studying spiritual wisdom.
- In a reading about love, this card may represent a relationship that contains a strong spiritual or magickal element. You and a partner may be on a spiritual path together, encouraging and inspiring one another.

### Reversed

The Magician reversed suggests you may be experiencing self-doubt or you can't yet see the way clearly. Perhaps you haven't fully developed the skills, knowledge, or confidence you need to take on a challenge or to follow the course you've chosen. Continue strengthening your latent power and wait until the time is ripe. Sometimes The Magician reversed can indicate your energy is too low now to accomplish your objective.

- In a reading about money, the reversed Magician can represent manipulation or using underhanded means for personal gain. Power struggles or deception may cause losses or setbacks.
- If the reading is about your job, watch your back—someone may be working behind the scenes to gain power or control. This card can also suggest hidden factors in your workplace that you're not aware of yet. Remain watchful and play your cards close to your chest.
- In a reading about love, you (or a partner) may be engaging in power struggles or manipulative behavior. This card can also represent deception or keeping secrets. In some cases, the reversed Magician means you're lonely and tired of a solo existence.

# THE HIGH PRIESTESS: 2

*Keywords: Intuition, emotions, feminine power, imagination, spirituality, the inner life*

This beautiful and enigmatic card symbolizes feminine spiritual power, or the Goddess from whom all life comes and to whom it all returns. Some decks show her as a serene female figure, seated with a book or scroll on her lap to indicate wisdom. Other decks depict her gazing into the distance at something yet to be revealed. She's sometimes positioned between two pillars—one black, one white—which represent the dual nature of existence: good and evil, light and dark, truth and deception, positive and negative.

> *"We all come from the Goddess*
> *And to her we shall return*
> *Like a drop of rain*
> *Flowing to the ocean."*
>
> —Zsuzsanna Budapest, American author

## Upright

The High Priestess may advise paying attention to your inner world—dreams, imagination, and intuition—especially if you tend to be a logical, practical person. Look more deeply at your hidden talents and motivations, face your "shadow," and reconcile your inner life with your outer one. Upright, The High Priestess suggests inner changes are taking place even if they haven't materialized yet. Something hidden is about to come forth.

---

### The Shadow

Psychologist Carl G. Jung thought The High Priestess symbolized "the shadow," the unknown, secret, dark, and mysterious part that lies within each of us.

---

- In a reading about money, you may be too "otherworldly" or impractical in financial areas; perhaps you need to get a handle on spending. The High Priestess can also advise listening to your intuition in an issue involving money.
- If the reading is about your job, this card recommends tuning in to "the invisible world" and taking advantage of your inner knowing and the spiritual guidance available to you. It can also mean working in a field that uses your inner power, intuition, and wisdom, such as psychology, holistic healing, or a spiritual path.
- In a reading about love, The High Priestess may describe a person who's intuitive, spiritual, in touch with the higher realms of existence. She can also represent a very romantic relationship that may not be well grounded in reality.

### Reversed

The High Priestess reversed says your unrealized potential has yet to be discovered—your secret, authentic self is locked away in the basement. Perhaps you're hesitant to look too deeply into yourself. Or, you may be hiding your true self from others because you fear their judgment or disapproval. In some cases, she means you're too involved in your inner world and need to get outside of yourself.

- In a reading about money, The High Priestess reversed can mean you're focused on money and the material world, at the expense of your inner life. Conversely, she may warn that you've got your head in the clouds—maybe you're ignoring a financial problem or expect someone to take care of you financially.
- If the reading is about your job, this card can mean your insecurities are holding you back. Or, it may recommend retreating from the busyness of everyday life—spend more time meditating or in spiritual practice. In some cases, it warns of treachery, secrets, or intrigue in your workplace—something hidden may soon come to light.
- In a reading about love, perhaps you or your partner is trying to hide something that needs to be revealed. Or, you may refuse to engage fully in a relationship. Sometimes this card symbolizes loneliness or withdrawal from close personal relationships.

# THE EMPRESS: 3

*Keywords: Creativity, feminine power, mature women, fertility, pleasure*

The Empress symbolizes feminine power in the material world, in contrast to The High Priestess, who represents feminine spiritual power. A card of beauty and creativity, The Empress is depicted as the Universal Mother who governs procreation, nurturing, the security and comforts of home, and domestic harmony. She's usually shown as a mature female figure, sometimes seated on a throne, sometimes in nature surrounded by flowers and vegetation indicating fruitfulness. The Empress is linked to Venus, the goddess of love, beauty, and pleasure—and some tarot decks include the astrological glyph for the planet on this card.

> *"The Lady is the Goddess, the feminine energy behind manifest nature, the bestower of fertility and creativity who brings all seeds to fruition."*
> —ANNA FRANKLIN, *THE SACRED CIRCLE TAROT*

## Upright

The Empress represents strong feminine energy and may describe a mother figure or a mature artistic/creative person. Whether she rules the home or a business, she represents female authority. A card of fertility, she signifies abundance of all kinds and shows your capacity for nurturing, caring, and supporting others as well as yourself. Sometimes this card refers to your own mother. In a man's reading, The Empress may encourage him to recognize the feminine component in himself.

### The Need for Love

When The Empress appears, ask yourself these questions: How do you show love and caring? Where do you express your creativity? What nurtures you? Is there a situation in your life where support or caretaking is needed?

- In a reading about money, The Empress indicates good fortune and success—you possess abundant resources and know how to use them productively. She can also recommend joining resources with a partner or group to increase financial gains.
- If the reading is about work, you're involved in a creative project and giving it your all—and success is likely. She may show that you've got things under control or advise you to take charge and work congenially toward a common goal. The Empress's message to you is find harmony, unite disparate factors, and reconcile differences for the good of all.
- In a reading about love, this card symbolizes a mature, loving relationship based on mutual respect, trust, and affection. It also indicates a powerful sexual connection. In some cases, The Empress may refer to a pregnancy or the desire for a pregnancy.

*"I, with a deeper instinct, choose a man who compels my strength, who makes enormous demands on me, who does not doubt my courage or my toughness, who does not believe me naïve or innocent, who has the courage to treat me like a woman."*

—ANAÏS NIN, *DELTA OF VENUS*

### Reversed

The Empress reversed reminds you to nurture yourself. Have you been spending too much time caring for others? Are other people's demands wearing you out? Are you neglecting your own personal needs? This is the card of the exhausted woman who's trying to balance a full-time career with caring for children and her home. Perhaps you need to develop your creative abilities. Claim your own power, instead of letting someone else define or control you.

- In a reading about money, the reversed Empress can indicate indulgence, overspending on luxuries, or greed. Conversely, she may mean you're lazy or slipshod when it comes to earning a living, or that you're too generous with other people.
- If the reading is about your job, this card suggests lack of confidence in your abilities may hold you back. Perhaps you feel thwarted, unvalued, stuck in a dull job where you can't use your creativity. Sometimes

this Empress represents someone who doesn't play nice with others or won't cooperate at work.

- In a reading about love, you may be giving too much or shouldering more than your share of the responsibilities in the relationship. Strike a balance between your needs and your partner's. In some cases, this card can show disinterest in sex, infertility, or infidelity.

# THE EMPEROR: 4

*Keywords: Leadership, masculine power, mature men, material success*

THE EMPEROR.

As his title suggests, The Emperor is a figure of supreme authority. He's usually shown as a mature man seated on a throne, as a warrior bearing a shield and sword, or outdoors where he wields power in the natural world. In some decks he wears royal robes and a crown, in others a suit of armor to signify his position of strength. Clearly he's a figure to be reckoned with. He's the savvy executive, the brave warrior, the responsible civic leader who has reached the summit of authority and achieved worldly power. The Emperor is an archetypal father figure, just as The Empress is a mother figure.

## The Head of a Ram

In the Rider-Waite-Smith deck, rams' heads appear on The Emperor's throne. These represent masculine power. In astrology, the ram is the symbol for the cardinal fire sign Aries, ruled by the planet Mars, which governs men. The Emperor also wears a red robe; red is the color associated with Mars and Aries.

## *Upright*

When The Emperor appears in a reading, look for issues related to authority. Although The Emperor represents worldly power, he's not a

*The Modern Witchcraft Book of Tarot*

despot or tyrant—he wants the best for everyone. He's a symbol of responsibility, intelligence, and courage who fights for what he believes in. As such, he's a protective male figure who teaches how to govern wisely in this world. He may also describe your own father and your relationship to him.

- In a reading about money, you possess the resources and savvy to succeed financially. You're good at making and managing money—you may even work in a financial field. The Emperor can represent success in a business or legal matter.
- If the reading is about your job, The Emperor shows you're handling responsibilities in professional life successfully. You're a capable, confident leader, and other people look up to you. You strive to produce something of lasting value and importance in the material world. Sometimes this card encourages you to become the authority, to take charge rather than following someone else's rule.
- In a reading about love, The Emperor symbolizes a mature, stable relationship, perhaps one based more on practical concerns, money, or status than passion. He indicates loyalty and commitment in a partnership.

### Reversed

If The Emperor is reversed, you may be in conflict with the established order—perhaps at your job, or with your family, religion, or ethnic group. This card can represent a person who's overbearing, chauvinistic, or self-righteous—or, conversely, one who's cowardly, indecisive, or lacks confidence. Sometimes it shows a loss of power or status and subsequent feelings of weakness or vulnerability.

- In a reading about money, you may lack the acumen to make or manage money successfully. Or, a lack of self-confidence may prevent you from getting ahead financially. Sometimes this card shows a situation in which you must stand up to adversaries and protect what's yours.
- If the reading is about your job, you may feel pressured to accept responsibilities you don't want or don't feel capable of handling. Perhaps you've lost a job through downsizing, or you lack the energy required to reach your goals. This card can indicate a need for more experience, drive,

or skill. If you're trying to please someone else or fit a role that's been dictated to you, it may be time to take the reins yourself.

- In a reading about love, this card suggests coldness, criticism, or an overly controlling nature. One person in the relationship is the boss who calls all the shots. Sometimes the reversed Emperor shows immaturity, lack of commitment, or infertility.

*"Be aware of stifling and stagnating rules and regulations . . . Learn when it is time to question the obligations and mores of society."*
—BARBARA MOORE, *THE GILDED TAROT COMPANION*

# THE HIEROPHANT: 5

*Keywords: Spiritual authority, leadership, tradition, institutions*

The Hierophant is a figure of authority and power, like The Emperor, but The Hierophant's power is of a spiritual nature. Often he's shown as a religious leader, and some decks call him The Pope. Sometimes he's seated on a throne, dressed in priestly raiment, crowned, and holding a scepter. In the Rider-Waite-Smith deck, acolytes stand before him, deferring to his wisdom as a representative of religious authority. He may represent a person who's dedicated to a religion or philosophy. Or, he can indicate that you're trying to break away from religious influence or dictates. In a broad sense, this card can refer to *any* organized institution, religious or otherwise, that exerts authority over its followers.

### Upright

Upright, The Hierophant says you choose to live according to the beliefs you share with a group or organization. It serves you in many ways—you derive security from knowing the rules and where you fit

*The Modern Witchcraft Book of Tarot*

in. Allying yourself with this group helps you achieve your goals. You might even be the leader, aspire to assume that position, or have a close relationship with the leader.

- In a reading about money, you probably hold traditional ideas about money and resources. Perhaps you could profit from allying yourself with an established group or a religious organization. Sometimes this card suggests paying more attention to spiritual considerations instead of being so focused on material matters.
- If the reading is about your job, The Hierophant indicates you must follow the rules if you want to succeed. Sometimes he represents a rigid corporate structure, religious organization, or educational system. Or, you may hold a position that uses your spiritual knowledge and interests.
- In a reading about love, this card may signify a relationship based on traditions, structure, or a spiritual path. You and a partner may be dedicated to serving a higher cause, and your relationship supports your goal.

### Keys to the Mysteries

The Rider-Waite-Smith deck shows two crossed keys below The Hierophant. These mark him as a teacher who holds the keys to the sacred mysteries. The keys also represent the intellect and intuition, and the need to use them in tandem.

## Reversed

If The Hierophant is reversed, it shows you're assessing your position. You may long to break away from an old tradition—religious, ideological, intellectual, or cultural—that no longer serves your needs. You want to live by whatever philosophy or belief structure resonates with your true nature, even if this puts you into conflict with others. Perhaps your faith is being challenged in some way and you must re-evaluate things you've taken for granted until now in order to be your own person.

> *"When the experience of the breath of God becomes morality, and morality becomes legality, and legality becomes a system of outer customs and conventions—then the process of degeneration lies unveiled before us."*
> —VALENTIN TOMBERG, *COVENANT OF THE HEART*

- In a reading about money, you may reject the material world to follow a spiritual path. Conversely, this card can indicate arrogance in financial areas and an attitude that you don't need to play by the rules because you're above all that.
- If the reading is about your job, you're probably questioning authority or the limitations in your workplace. Sometimes the reversed Hierophant indicates leaving an organization that you feel is unprincipled or that doesn't hold your values.
- In a reading about love, the reversed Hierophant may mean you feel trapped in a relationship because you're afraid to buck a social, religious, or cultural order. This card can also indicate a relationship in which one person holds most of the power or is judgmental or dogmatic.

# THE LOVERS: 6

*Keywords: Partnership, union of opposites, choices, harmony, cooperation*

THE LOVERS.

The Lovers card usually shows a man and woman, but there the similarities end. In some decks they're naked, in others they're clothed. Some decks show the couple touching—even engaged in a passionate embrace—whereas others place them on opposite sides of the card, perhaps with a winged being overlooking them á la the Garden of Eden. You'll even find decks that present three people on the card, as if a third party—who might be a young person or an older parental figure—is influencing their relationship. Although many people interpret this card as representing romantic love, it's really about the union of opposites, often expressed as the union of the male and female sides of your own dual nature. That doesn't rule out romance in your future if The Lovers shows up in a reading; it just means *union* has many meanings other than male-female coupling.

*The Modern Witchcraft Book of Tarot*

In mythology, The Lovers reflects Eros, the son of Aphrodite, the Greek goddess of love and beauty. The Romans called him Cupid, and it was his job to shoot the arrows of love, considered a form of madness, at unsuspecting youths. Thus, the Greeks often depicted Eros blindfolded to represent that "love is blind." But Eros has another role—to guide us toward our true destiny, which is to say, "Do what you love, and everything else will follow naturally."

## Upright

This is a card of cooperation, of working together with others to accomplish a joint purpose. When it appears upright, it signifies an attraction and partnership of some kind, not only the romantic variety. It can also suggest you're uniting disparate parts of yourself. The Lovers represents a period of harmony, in personal or professional matters. Sometimes it indicates you need to make a choice between two things you value, but you'll make the right decision.

- In a reading about money, you can profit from combining your resources with someone else's. Sometimes The Lovers symbolizes benefitting from a partner's money or marrying into wealth. If you're seeking a financial backer, this card gives you a thumbs-up.
- If the reading is about your job, this card represents a time of cooperation, contentment, and harmony. Joint projects are favored now. Two forces have united toward a common goal. The Lovers can also signify meeting a partner through work or working with a romantic partner in a business.
- In a reading about love, this card bodes well for a romantic relationship. It shows mutual caring and attraction, a rewarding partnership that brings out the best in both people. Sometimes it means a decision in connection with a love relationship.

## Reversed

Reversed, The Lovers may indicate conflict, discontent, or separation from a person—or within yourself. You feel unable to connect with the object of your desire, whether that's a flesh-and-blood lover or something you feel passionate about, and this causes unhappiness. Perhaps you feel unable to express your love or believe if you do, you'll be rejected. The card can also show you're uncertain about a decision you must make or unhappy with the outcome of a choice you've already made.

- In a reading about money, this card can represent a financial partnership falling apart. A backer may withdraw support, or a joint venture may not get off the ground. Perhaps you're struggling with a choice or lamenting a bad decision.
- If the reading is about your job, this card may indicate a delay or warn that you're trying to force cooperation between incompatible elements. Disagreements, lack of cooperation, or arguments may cause problems in your workplace.
- In a reading about love, The Lovers reversed can indicate you and a lover are separated by circumstances: location, responsibilities, or even death (no, it doesn't mean a partner will die, but it can symbolize a lover who's gone to the Other Side and how you're dealing with this). Sometimes it represents manipulation, a loveless relationship, incompatibility, or quarreling. It can also encourage you to heal an inner rift.

*"Can you make someone love you? No. Can you make yourself love someone else? Not much. Can you live without either being loved or loving a partner? It is probably the hardest task on this earth, but you can, and in the long run clearing your closets of relationships that no longer work is frightening but an utter necessity. The worst thing that can happen is you are the only one left in the equation, and you must learn to love yourself."*
—JANE STERN, *CONFESSIONS OF A TAROT READER*

## Love and Magick

In myth, song, and poetry, love and magick are often linked. When we speak of falling in love, we use such terms as *enchanted, charmed, bewitched, under a lover's spell*—and it often feels that way. But as Shakespeare wrote in his delightful play about magick and love, *A Midsummer Night's Dream*, "The course of true love never did run smooth." Therefore, it's probably no surprise that the most frequently cast spells are—you guessed it—love spells. The Lovers card can play a colorful role in love spells, as you'll see in Part IV of this book.

*The Modern Witchcraft Book of Tarot*

# THE CHARIOT: 7

*Keywords: Controlling opposing forces, willpower, resolving conflict, travel*

The Chariot often depicts a strong male figure holding the reins of two horses or sphinx-like beasts, one black and one white, signifying opposing forces. Sometimes the beasts are unicorns or other mythical creatures like Pegasus, the winged horse, or griffins. In the Rider-Waite-Smith deck, the charioteer is armored and carries a scepter, suggesting he is in the service of royalty. In some decks, he holds no reins—he uses sheer willpower to keep his steeds moving together in a forward direction. This shows mastery of opposing forces and control over inner conflicts. At a literal level, The Chariot relates to travel and transportation.

---

### The Wheel of the Year

In Aleister Crowley's Thoth Tarot, the charioteer holds a large disc or wheel in front of him. That and the wheels on his chariot represent the ever-changing cycles of life and nature. Witches may see these as symbols of the Wheel of the Year. The four sphinxes pulling the chariot represent the four elements.

---

## Upright

Upright, The Chariot symbolizes taking control of competing forces—whether these are inner conflicts, people, or a situation in your life—in order to reach your goals. You're being carried toward your destination as quickly as possible. Whatever the task, you can handle it. You're keeping up with the changes that are happening—at your job, in a relationship, or in some type of community or worldly involvement.

- In a reading about money, this card says you can't rush things. All you can do is hold on to the reins and guide the situation, using your willpower and mastery to bring a financial matter to a successful conclusion.

- If the reading is about your job, The Chariot reminds you that to succeed you need *self-mastery*. You possess the means to triumph over obstacles and stay the course you've set for yourself. You're holding things together successfully, uniting opposing forces to stay on track. However, you may be required to make frequent adjustments to continue going in the right direction.
- In a reading about love, this card recommends spending time in self-development rather than chasing after love. This may not be the right time to start a romance. If you're in a relationship already, you may need to take control of conflicting feelings or attitudes to bring about harmony.

### Reversed

The Chariot reversed says changes are happening so fast you feel out of control. It may seem like you're being pulled in two directions at once, and the stress is intense. You fear you won't be able to control the multiple factors of a given situation. You're at a crossroads—choose your direction carefully. The more you can tune in to your own inner guidance, the more control you can exert outwardly. Most likely, the solution to the problem at hand is to take the middle road between the conflicting issues.

- In a reading about money, you could suffer setbacks or losses due to confusion, indecision, or inattentiveness. Lack of confidence or inexperience could result in a poor choice. Or, you may rush into a financial matter unprepared and run headlong into a wall.
- If the reading is about your job, competing factions may cause stress in your workplace and you feel incapable of controlling the situation. Or, things may be happening so fast your head is spinning and you can't get your bearings. Sometimes this card says you're being pulled in two different directions and can't decide which one to take.
- In a reading about love, conflicts or differences in opinion, lifestyle, or values cause tension in a relationship. Or, a change has thrown you off-guard and you don't know how to handle the situation. Sometimes this card represents romantic involvement with two different people or a conflict between two things you love.

# STRENGTH: 8

*Keywords: Inner power, overcoming weaknesses, courage, persistence*

STRENGTH.

Some tarot artists show Strength as a woman in relationship to a lion. The woman seems to be controlling the powerful beast—even treating him affectionately as she would a pet. In the Rider-Waite-Smith deck, the woman bends over the lion, gently closing his jaws as if she expects no resistance to her touch. In other decks, she caresses the lion, rides atop him, or stands beside him. Although some interpreters view this card as emblematic of the struggle with your "animal" nature, others see it as symbolic of self-confidence and inner strength, of being in harmony with your instinctive nature.

---

### Strength's Number

Some decks assign Strength the number eleven and give Justice number eight. I think Strength and eight are more closely aligned—and so did the creators of the Rider-Waite-Smith deck, who broke with the older numbering system. From the perspective of numerology, eight corresponds to pragmatism, material mastery, and financial success, whereas eleven represents humanitarianism and equality.

---

## *Upright*

Strength shows you're exhibiting moral courage and fortitude. You've learned to work with your instinctive nature, to listen to it and hear its whisperings. In shamanic teachings and mythology, animals often serve as guides and teachers who help us on our way. This card indicates you've come through difficulties and learned to rely on inner strength to solve problems. You've grown strong through suffering trials and tribulations—you've tamed the "beast" within. The lesson of this card is we don't conquer our animal natures by brute force but by gentleness and feeling our way into rapport with the instinctive side.

- In a reading about money, you have the inner resources necessary to succeed. Strength can mean you're in a strong position financially or that a venture is sound. Sometimes this card advises you to rely on yourself, not others, and to trust your instincts.
- If the reading is about your job, Strength shows that challenges have led you to discover your inner strength. Use this strength to overcome obstacles—you can handle whatever comes your way. Because you've learned to listen to both logic and intuition, the decisions you make and the actions you take will succeed.
- In a reading about love, this card can indicate you've befriended your instinctual side; now your inner drives are in harmony with your outer desires. It can also suggest being patient and gentle with a partner and/or yourself as you forge a strong relationship.

### Reversed

When Strength shows up reversed, it suggests a struggle between your inner and outer selves. Either you're being controlled by your emotions and your "animal nature" or you're ignoring your instincts and listening only to logic. Brute force alone won't get you where you want to go. Set your ego aside for now.

- In a reading about money, inner fears, insecurity, or indecision may be interfering with your prosperity. Or, you may be using the wrong means to gain financially. Listen to your instincts as well as your intellect to avoid setbacks.
- If the reading is about your job, you may feel overwhelmed by a situation or uncertain how to handle it. Lack of confidence keeps you from achieving your goals. This card can also mean you're trying to muscle your way ahead, which will likely fail. Your position may not be as strong as you think.
- In a reading about love, you may be afraid to show your true feelings and put up a tough façade. However, this won't bring the happiness you seek. Relinquish your defenses, put your ego aside, and open your heart to make a relationship work.

# THE HERMIT: 9

*Keywords: Guidance, solitude, inner wisdom, self-evaluation*

The Hermit is often depicted as a bearded old man holding a lantern aloft. A seeker after truth, he lights the way ahead for those who follow. He may look like a monk dressed in a plain, long robe. An archetypal elder figure, the sage of myth and legend, he radiates wisdom and functions as a teacher and guide. Sometimes he's shown looking away at what only he can see—your future.

When The Hermit appears in a reading, it can mean a guide figure is at hand, offering help. The card advises you to meet this guide or begin your own search for truth. Sometimes, the guide figure is a person—such as a counselor, therapist, or clergy member—but usually it refers to inner guidance, or getting in touch with a spirit guide. The Hermit can recommend withdrawing from the busyness and distractions of the outer world to do some soul-searching.

## Father Time

The Hermit is often linked with Father Time, or Saturn—the planet astrologers connect with obstacles and lessons that come up during the course of our lives. As such, he reminds you to be patient and brutally honest with yourself as you work to gain perspective.

## *Upright*

Remember the saying, "When the student is ready, the teacher appears"? When this card is upright, you may be looking for guidance from the invisible world. You want to gain perspective on your life, and you're open to the inner guidance that's available to you. The time has come to reunite with the Source, whether for guidance, to discover the truth, or to establish inner balance.

- In a reading about money, The Hermit offers guidance in a financial matter. He may encourage you to seek counsel from someone wiser or more experienced than yourself. Sometimes this card represents turning away from material things to follow a spiritual path.
- If the reading is about your job, The Hermit may indicate withdrawing from the hectic pace of the workaday world—you seek solitude, wisdom, and inner peace. This card can also mean leaving a job or company and going your own way, independently.
- In a reading about love, you may feel a need for some time alone to discover things about yourself and your path in life. The Hermit can also indicate a need for more independence or self-reliance in a relationship.

*"If the doors of perception were cleansed, every thing would appear to man as it is, infinite."*

—WILLIAM BLAKE

### Reversed

Reversed, The Hermit suggests you're ignoring or rejecting the wisdom being offered to you. It's time—or long past time—for self-evaluation. Reflect on your hopes and goals, your associations, your relationships, your career, and your purpose in life. Sometimes this card shows you don't want to be alone and feel sad, frightened, or isolated.

- In a reading about money, you may be unwilling to look at a financial matter closely or reluctant to listen to advice. Sometimes this card suggests you're overly cautious, and that's limiting you. It can also mean rejecting the material world for the spiritual one.
- If the reading is about your job, you need to withdraw to think things through, to sort out your life and the issues confronting you. Keeping busy can be a form of denial. Sometimes the reversed Hermit indicates being forced to leave a secure job and go it alone.
- In a reading about love, you may try to fill your time with social activity to avoid facing yourself. In some cases, The Hermit reversed may mean disappointment in a romantic situation or leaving a relationship that no longer fulfills you.

*The Modern Witchcraft Book of Tarot*

# WHEEL OF FORTUNE: 10

*Keywords: Change, destiny, unexpected turn of events, good luck*

WHEEL of FORTUNE.

Some decks depict the Wheel of Fortune with eight spokes, a reference to the eight pagan sabbats or holidays that mark the sun's annual passage across the sky and the ever-turning cycles of life. Other decks show human or mythical figures attached to the wheel, indicating we're all tied to the wheel of time and subject to life's ups and downs. The Rider-Waite-Smith deck includes winged versions of astrological symbols, which represent the four elements, in the card's corners, suggesting the influence of divine forces.

Consciously or unconsciously, you've put something in motion and you now have little or no control over the outcome. A new phase in your life is beginning, an important decision must be made, or an upcoming circumstance will change your life. Destiny is at work, and you have to accept whatever happens. All you can do is attune yourself to the forces operating now.

---

### The Moirai

The Wheel of Fortune is linked to the three Fates, collectively called the Moirai in Greek mythology. One spins the thread of life, the second weaves it, and the third cuts it. Thus, the Wheel of Fortune is a reminder of the mysterious cycles of life, death, and rebirth, and of the invisible forces that measure them out to each of us.

---

## *Upright*

A favorable outcome awaits you. Circumstances are changing for the better. Even if you aren't totally aware of what you've done to initiate the process, you've started the ball rolling—or rather, the wheel turning.

Don't resist—these changes will promote growth and bring valuable learning experiences for you. It can be hard to stay balanced, but go with the flow and trust the process.

- In a reading about money, this card heralds good fortune coming your way as a result of what you've already put into motion. Perhaps through a stroke of "good luck" your finances improve. Seize opportunities that present themselves.
- If the reading is about your job, you may get a lucky break. Unexpected turns of events are likely, such as meeting people who can help you or receiving an offer "out of the blue." Although this may appear fortuitous, it's all part of the grand plan for your life.
- In a reading about love, a new romance may begin or an existing relationship may improve—even if you don't think you've done anything to make that happen. The time is right for this change. Enjoy it.

---

### The Wiccan Rede

The Wheel of Fortune is often linked with karma, which Wiccans describe in what's known as the Wiccan Rede:

*Bide the Wiccan law ye must,*
*In perfect love and perfect trust,*
*Eight words the Wiccan Rede fulfill:*
*An' ye harm none, do what ye will.*
*What ye send forth comes back to thee,*
*So ever mind the Rule of Three.*
*Follow this with mind and heart,*
*And merry ye meet, and merry ye part.*

---

## Reversed

Reversed, the Wheel of Fortune can indicate losses or that a situation will turn out badly. More often, it suggests you're trying to avoid your destiny, refusing to make the necessary changes or take the required actions. Fear of the unknown is blocking you, and this is causing stagnation and frustration. It's time to "take the wheel" and do what you know you need to do.

*The Modern Witchcraft Book of Tarot*

- In a reading about money, the reversed Wheel can indicate ups and downs in your finances. An investment may be unstable, or fear may cause you to miss an opportunity. Perhaps the time simply isn't right for big gains—be patient, but remain alert.
- If the reading is about your job, you may experience delays or disappointments because you lack commitment. A job change may not be advantageous now—either you're not prepared to make this move or the position you're considering isn't stable.
- In a reading about love, you may experience delays in establishing a relationship, perhaps because the time isn't right. This card can also signify a turn for the worse in a partnership, although it may be only temporary.

# JUSTICE: 11

*Keywords: Rectification, decision, finding balance, legal matters*

The Justice card often depicts a female figure, robed and crowned, or sometimes armored. She holds a sword (symbol of the air element and the mind) in one hand, and in the other a set of scales. In some decks, she appears nude with arms outstretched in a balanced position, or she stands between a large set of scales while holding a smaller set. This Justice isn't blind (or blindfolded), however; her eyes are open, suggesting divine justice is at work here rather than the laws of humankind. The Justice card can represent an actual legal matter or someone who works in the judicial system. Whatever the situation, you must weigh many factors in order to make a reasoned decision.

### Upright

The Justice card tells you to look to your inner self for guidance—don't rely solely on human advisers. Deliberate calmly and carefully—weigh all the factors—before taking action or reaching a decision. If you're involved in a legal matter and Justice appears upright, you can expect things to proceed smoothly, fairly, and in an objective manner. Sometimes Justice says you need to right a wrong or rectify a matter. A card of karma, it suggests you're reaping what you've sown. Or, it may advise you to become more balanced, temperate, or fair-minded.

- In a reading about money, Justice upright can symbolize a legal matter in which property is divided equitably or a fair financial settlement is reached. It can also mean sharing wealth or earning money through honest means.
- If the reading is about your job, Justice can mean reaching an amicable agreement or signing a contract. This card upright can also represent a time of cooperation and harmony, when problems can be resolved. Seek an equitable division of labor, responsibilities, and rewards.
- In a reading about love, this card advises you to seek balance and fairness in a relationship. One of you may need to adjust your behavior to create a more equitable situation. Sometimes Justice indicates a contractual agreement or legal arrangement, such as marriage.

---

### The Goddess Maat

Justice has ties to the Egyptian goddess Maat, whose name means truth and justice. She held a pair of scales upon which she weighed a newly dead person's soul against the Feather of Truth to decide if the soul was worthy to pass into the realm of Osiris, god of the underworld.

---

### Reversed

Justice reversed indicates delays in legal matters or unfairness in some other situation. If you're the person in power, you may be unduly severe in meting out punishment. If you're in the powerless position, you may feel angry or resentful at being treated unfairly. Your equilibrium is out of whack, and you may swing from one extreme to another.

- In a reading about money, you may encounter a loss in a legal matter or feel a financial decision isn't fair. Perhaps you'll be required to

*The Modern Witchcraft Book of Tarot*

make restitution to someone. This card can also represent delays or complications in receiving money that's due to you.

- If the reading is about your job, Justice reversed can signify an imbalance in your workplace or a lack of cooperation. Or, this card may mean you have to account for an action or mistake. In some cases, it may point to a legal issue involving the organization you work for.
- In a reading about love, you may feel a relationship lacks balance—one of you has more power or control than the other. Sometimes this card indicates having to answer for an indiscretion or wrongful action.

# THE HANGED MAN: 12

*Keywords: Letting go, surrender, seeing things from a different perspective, sacrifice*

The Hanged Man usually hangs upside down by one leg, although this doesn't seem to bother him—he appears quite nonchalant. In the Rider-Waite-Smith deck, he's suspended from the branch of a tree, which may represent the Tree of Life or the World Tree. When this card appears in a reading, it can mean surrendering to a situation, letting go of old patterns or attitudes. You're ready to make sacrifices in order to be true to yourself. Something may have turned your world upside down, but now you have an opportunity to see things from a different perspective.

### Upright

You feel suspended between the past and the future—a new direction is in the making. Although it can be difficult to let go of old patterns, people, and things that give you security, The Hanged Man says letting go is essential to your continued growth. Perhaps it's time to sacrifice superficial pleasures for a more spiritual way of life. You may have gone through a major transformation that's shaken up your old way of life and made you realize there's more to life than material goods, worldly success, and physical reality. The Hanged Man can also recommend looking at things from a different perspective—what do you see when you turn the picture upside down?

- In a reading about money, this card may mean you've chosen to follow a less materialistic way of life. You may divest yourself of money and possessions, or simply change the way you think about money. Sometimes The Hanged Man indicates a loss that frees you to move forward in life without old attachments.
- If the reading is about your job, you need to make a change, but the good news is there's no hurry. Take your time and make the right decisions about what you truly want, now and in the long term. Step outside the box and try to look at things in a new way.
- In a reading about love, you (or your partner) may need to relinquish control and set aside your ego for the good of the relationship. Try to view the situation in a different way. The Hanged Man can indicate you are leaving a relationship that no longer holds meaning for you.

*"He hangs upside down partly because he has turned around society's values, and partly because of the yogic and alchemical practise of reversing the body to allow energy to travel from the base of the spine to the brain—the unconscious made conscious."*

—RACHEL POLLACK, *SALVADOR DALI'S TAROT*

## Odin, the Hanged Man

We see a connection between The Hanged Man and the Norse god Odin who hung on the great tree Yggdrasil for nine days, during which he gained the wisdom of the runes. Some tarotists see The Hanged Man as representing self-sacrifice and martyrdom—they even link it with the Crucifixion and connect the tree with the cross. Others view it as voluntary surrender to the process of achieving enlightenment.

## Reversed

You're at a crossroads but can't make a decision—you're just swinging in the breeze. To move forward, you must spend time in spiritual development—but you may not be willing to do that. Perhaps you're not paying attention to your real needs and this is causing frustration. Ask yourself a few questions: Are you sacrificing some part of yourself unnecessarily or refusing to sacrifice what really needs to go? Are you unable to see a matter clearly? Are you "hung up" about something? Are you being true to yourself?

- In a reading about money, this card can mean you're clinging to materialistic ideas when you really should work on spiritual development. Sometimes The Hanged Man reversed warns you could be headed for a loss if you don't willingly let go of the past.
- If the reading is about your work, you may feel tied to a job you don't like or that's going nowhere because you're unwilling to make a change. Or, you may lack direction or motivation—instead of seeking the work that's right for you, you're just "hanging out."
- In a reading about love, you may cling to a relationship you've outgrown instead of making a change. Or, you're "hung up" on someone who doesn't return your affection. Perhaps you're unwilling to sacrifice a habit or behavior for the good of the relationship.

*"You are that which you are seeking."*

—SAINT FRANCIS OF ASSISI

# DEATH: 13

*Keywords: Transformation, metamorphosis, an ending, sacrifice, loss and rebirth*

The Death card tends to frighten people when it comes up in a reading, but although it looks scary, it symbolizes a transformation at work. It rarely predicts physical death, although it may reference a death or loss that has led to a transformation for you. Some decks picture a "Grim Reaper" skeleton with a scythe, grinning toothily and wearing a black hooded robe. The Rider-Waite-Smith deck shows a skeleton in black armor riding a white charger, suggesting the ongoing cycles of life and death. Other decks show desolate landscapes, severed body parts lying around, and other disturbing imagery, but you shouldn't take this literally. Remember, the tarot is jam-packed with symbols that can only be understood metaphorically.

---

### The Number of Death

The Death card's number thirteen has all sorts of symbolism attached to it. Some people link it with the thirteen men at the Last Supper. Thirteen also corresponds to the number of lunar months in a year and the transformation from a lunar calendar (and the decline of matriarchal societies) to a solar calendar (and the ascension of patriarchal societies).

---

## *Upright*

The Death card signifies the end, or death, of a cycle. Whenever a stage in life ends, you need to mourn it. Trying desperately to hold on to what's clearly over causes trouble. Jobs end, relationships end, children grow up and move away from home. Change can't be avoided. The ultimate message of the Death card is the promise that new life follows disintegration. You're experiencing a metamorphosis: think caterpillar to butterfly.

*The Modern Witchcraft Book of Tarot*

- In a reading about money, you may need to let go of old attitudes about money or change the way you've handled resources in the past. Death may also represent the end of one financial endeavor and the start of a new one.
- If the reading is about your work, this card symbolizes a transition in your career path, a job change, or a major shift in your work arena. Old, outworn conditions that have held you back are breaking down to make room for new growth.
- In a reading about love, Death says the patterns you once found workable are no longer effective. You and/or a partner may need to change the way you behave or interact with one another. Sometimes this card shows the end of an unsatisfactory relationship.

*"The Goddess has led the Fool to his death, because only through his spiritual death can he be renewed and come to rebirth. She has asked him to sacrifice his image of himself to find his true Self; the old self must be left behind or 'die' before a spiritual rebirth can take place. The frightening Cailleach or Crone is really the Wise Old Woman who guides him. She is the keeper of the mysteries."*
—ANNA FRANKLIN, *THE SACRED CIRCLE TAROT*

## Reversed

When this card appears reversed, it suggests you're putting off making necessary changes, usually out of fear. You're stuck in old habit patterns you know need to be revised, but you don't want to put forth the effort to alter them, even though you're unhappy with the current situation. The way out is to face up to your stagnation, frustration, and unhappiness. Throw out the old and ring in the new.

- In a reading about money, you may be unwilling to let go of a bad investment or fear taking a chance on something new. Perhaps irresponsible spending habits are undermining you. Although you worry about your financial stability, you refuse to make changes.
- If the reading is about your job, insecurity or fear may cause you to stay in a dead-end position, instead of cutting loose and moving on to something better. In some cases, this card may symbolize a job

that involves death, such as hospice, the funeral business, or estate planning.

- In a reading about love, you know your relationship needs work but resist making the necessary adjustments. As a result, you experience boredom, lethargy, or sadness. Sometimes this card indicates you're stuck in grieving the end of a relationship, unwilling to move on.

# TEMPERANCE: 14

*Keywords: Moderation, harmony, acceptance, resolution, cooperation, patience*

This lovely card often features a winged angel—male, female, or androgynous. In the Rider-Waite-Smith deck, the angel stands in a stream bordered by flowers. In some decks, the figure pours liquid—the elixir of life—from a golden vessel into a silver one in a continuous stream, suggesting the interplay of the material and spiritual worlds. The word *vessel* relates to the great mother god-

desses of antiquity, and the human body is often referred to as the "vessel of the soul." Thus, both the angelic figure and the cups are symbolic references to the feminine force.

## Upright

Upright, Temperance indicates a time of inner growth and outer harmony. You're learning to temper your ego needs with the needs of the spirit within. With patience, you can blend disparate elements of yourself and/or your world into a harmonious whole.

- In a reading about money, moderation is the key. Don't expect immediate gains or huge profits at this time. This card may indicate a period when your finances are balanced, or it may recommend getting money matters in order.

*The Modern Witchcraft Book of Tarot*

- If the reading is about your job, Temperance represents a time of cooperation and relative peace in your workplace. It can also recommend distributing responsibilities and rewards among coworkers in an equitable way. Sometimes this card tells you to balance work and play.
- In a reading about love, Temperance urges you to heal rifts, avoid ego struggles, and seek peace in a relationship. It can also advise you to let a relationship develop at its own pace—don't try to rush things.

## Patience in All Things

The word *temperance* derives from the Latin *temperare*, which means to moderate, blend, or mix together harmoniously. Interestingly, this card was named Time in early decks, which provides a key to its underlying meaning. Temperance encourages patience—things happen at their own pace, in their own time. This is one of the great lessons of the Zen masters. There are times when nothing *can* be done and nothing *needs* to be done.

## Reversed

When Temperance is reversed, a situation may be stalled or out of balance. All you can do is let matters work themselves out, which they will in time. Be patient—trying to force inharmonious factors together will only cause bad feelings and poor results, like mixing oil and water. Extreme actions or reactions will likely backfire now.

- In a reading about money, intemperate spending may have plunged you into debt. Conversely, insecurity or lack of self-worth may lead you to hoard money instead of enjoying it or finding ways to make it work for you.
- If the reading is about work, you may have trouble handling the responsibilities of your job or balancing your professional and personal life. Perhaps you're not using your time efficiently. Temperance reversed can also indicate lack of cooperation or discord in your workplace.
- In a reading about love, extreme emotions may provoke arguments or a standoff between you and a partner. Egos get in the way of harmony and happiness. Temperance reversed can mean trying to rush a relationship, which causes tension and frustration.

# THE DEVIL: 15

*Keywords: Obsession, indulgence, fear, materialism, egotism*

THE DEVIL .

Many decks picture a medieval Christian-type devil, complete with horns, hooves, a hairy tail, and a pitchfork. The Rider-Waite-Smith deck shows two small humanlike figures at the devil's feet, one male and one female, with chains around their necks that represent bondage to the material realm. Notice the chains are loose, though, and the people could easily slip them off, suggesting this card is about self-imposed limitations.

When you think of "the devil," what comes to your mind? Consummate evil? A mythical creature? A symbol of human indulgence, ignorance, egotism, greed, and irresponsibility? I think of The Devil as the "obsession card."

---

### The Horned God

The Devil appears to be one of the more alarming cards of the Major Arcana. However, he does not represent satanic forces or evil. That goatish guy is paganism's horned god Pan, connected to the fertility rites banned by the Christian church. Therefore, his appearance can indicate a sexual component to your question or concern. In the Thoth Tarot, Crowley's Devil is clearly phallic.

---

## Upright

When The Devil shows up in a reading, he recommends re-evaluating your relationship to people and material things that keep you "chained." It's time to let go of old fears, hang-ups, inhibitions, and ways you manipulate others to satisfy your needs. The Devil tells you to figure out what's true and what's false, at least for you.

- In a reading about money, this card can advise you to confront fears about financial security, social status, and material success. Are you too attached to money and material things? Are you taking advantage of others for personal gain? Are you "selling your soul to the devil" in order to profit?

- If the reading is about your work, The Devil may indicate you're chained to your job and neglecting other areas of life. Perhaps you're a workaholic or crave the status your position gives you. This card warns against engaging in questionable practices to get ahead.
- In a reading about love, The Devil asks, "Is an abusive, obsessive, or harmful relationship adversely affecting your life?" Sexual desire may cause you to overlook character flaws in a partner. Self-inflicted bondage is preventing you from moving ahead.

*"The Beast is always the dark face of the Handsome Prince."*
—LIZ GREENE, *SATURN: A NEW LOOK AT AN OLD DEVIL*

### Reversed
Reversed, The Devil indicates you feel trapped in a situation over which you think you have no control. You may believe your options are limited or blame someone else for your problems, but if you're honest with yourself, you'll see your own ideas and fears are causing the problem. Be careful of a "quick fix"—you probably need to do some serious work, both inner and outer, to solve the issues and move to a better place.

- In a reading about money, the reversed Devil suggests greed may cause you to engage in unethical practices or profit at other people's expense. Remember the saying, "Love of money is the root of all kinds of evil." Sometimes this card means someone else owns you due to indebtedness or your lust for money.
- If the reading is about your job, you may be a wage slave, prostituting yourself, afraid to break free. Perhaps you engage in self-destructive practices—working so hard you damage your health or allowing your employer to take advantage of you. The reversed Devil can also mean working for a corrupt organization or in a shady activity.
- In a reading about love, your self-esteem may be compromised by a relationship in which you're devalued. This card speaks of codependence, manipulation, delusion, and deception. Don't walk away—run!

# THE TOWER: 16

*Keywords: Change, freedom, upsets, destruction of the old*

The Tower usually depicts a fortresslike structure, similar to those remaining from medieval times in parts of Europe, being destroyed by fire or lightning. In some decks, including the Rider-Waite-Smith deck, the tower's crown is being blown off by the fiery impact. The blast catapults human figures out of the windows. Like the Death card and The Devil, The Tower tends to engender fear when it comes up in a reading. However, The Tower does not necessarily represent ruin and devastation, although its appearance usually does herald swift and dramatic change—sometimes shocking and extremely upsetting change. Many people interpret The Tower as signifying catastrophe, but whatever disruption or destruction it heralds is ultimately for the best.

---

### September 11

The Tower's graphic imagery played out in our own lives during the 9/11 attacks on the World Trade Center. That physical event depicts literally what the frightening card shows—something the tarot's early artists could not have imagined. The Tower often represents collapse of a social order or established system, and New York's twin towers were symbols of established wealth and power. In an instant, the attack changed the way Americans thought about their position in the world.

---

## *Upright*

When this card appears, it usually means you've ignored or denied something that's rotten and needs to be blown apart. You're probably surprised, but you shouldn't be. You knew changes were necessary, but you refused to take action. Then something happens—losing a job, the end of a relationship, an accident, a financial setback—that forces you to face reality. Bigtime. Your life is collapsing around you, but that old, worn-out structure had to go. The Tower demands you free yourself from the self-created fortress in which you've imprisoned yourself. In the wake of the chaos, a new order can grow.

- In a reading about money, this card heralds a major change in your finances. An unexpected loss or setback may cause you to reassess your attitudes about money—and perhaps free you from your attachment to wealth, status, possessions, and the related responsibilities.
- If the reading is about your work, The Tower may represent a sudden job loss or change in your workplace. Yes, you're shocked and feel the rug's been pulled out from under you, but this may be exactly what you need to escape the walls that trapped you.
- In a reading about love, this card suggests you need to overthrow false ideas, old habit patterns, and outdated ways of relating to a partner. A breakup or major change in a relationship is necessary and imminent; with it will come more freedom.

*"The collapse of the tower is echoed in description of shamanic initiation, where the candidate experiences, in a vision, a symbolic dismemberment whereby his body is stripped down to its bones."*
—Anna Franklin, *The Sacred Circle Tarot*

### Reversed
When The Tower appears reversed, you're refusing to change old habit patterns and will suffer continued disruption in the form of unforeseen difficulties until you finally get the message. At a deep level, you're being prepared for the changes that *must* eventually take place, but you're resisting what your inner self knows already. Once you alter limiting beliefs and behaviors, you'll experience a new sense of freedom in your life.

- In a reading about money, you may suffer unexpected losses or find yourself struggling to hold on to what you have. Perhaps you're in denial about the collapse that's taking place, hoping it's just a little "adjustment." It's also possible that you may see the light and escape the worst.

- If the reading is about your job, this card can mean you're clinging to old structures even as they crumble. Pressure and discomfort increase until you finally jump ship. If you continue to hold on, you may go down amid the flames and rubble.
- In a reading about love, you may resist making changes and, as a result, they may be thrust upon you. An affair begins suddenly, a partner leaves in a huff, a crisis destroys your happy home. You've ignored the warning signs; now you must deal with the aftermath.

## THE STAR: 17

*Keywords: Happiness, hope, light at the end of the tunnel, good fortune*

This lovely card often portrays a nude female figure in or beside a pool of water; in some decks, she pours water from two jugs or chalices. In the Rider-Waite-Smith deck, she pours the contents of one pitcher into a stream and the other onto the ground, showing the connection between the two feminine elements: water and earth. Stars shine in the background, sometimes in a circle or a halo-like formation around her. The naked woman represents truth and purity; the jugs contain the waters of life.

We see shooting stars as harbingers of good luck. We wish upon a star, for the star is a universal symbol of hope. Getting this card is like looking up at the bright starry sky on a clear night and seeing all the magnificence of the universe. This is a time of fulfillment, good fortune, creative inspiration, and spiritual growth, when you receive help from unseen forces and wishes come true.

*"Hope . . . which whispered from Pandora's box only after all the other plagues and sorrows had escaped, is the best and last of all things."*
—Ian Caldwell and Dustin Thomason, *The Rule of Four*

## Upright

The Star signals an end to problems and the start of a new, happier phase of life. I think of it as the "light at the end of the tunnel card." You've been preparing for this time and now you've arrived. The Star shows you're in harmony with your life purpose, using your gifts beneficially. It signifies inspiration, intuition, inner wisdom, and joy.

- In a reading about money, The Star signals an improvement in your financial position. Help comes from both the invisible world and the material one. Remain hopeful—your dreams can be achieved.
- If the reading is about your job, you may be moving into the spotlight, getting recognition for your efforts—you're the "star" and it's your turn to shine. You feel good about yourself and confident in your place in the universe. Success lies just around the corner.
- In a reading about love, this card represents a bright, beautiful relationship that inspires you and brings you joy. The wish you made has or will soon come true.

*"Optimism is the faith that leads to achievement. Nothing can be done without hope and confidence."*

—Helen Keller

## Reversed

Trust life and its processes—and yourself. The reversed Star can mean you're following your path in a private way, instead of shining your light into the outer world. The blessings you receive may be spiritual, rather than material. Perhaps you feel devitalized, uninspired, or low on self-esteem at this time. After you attune yourself to what your soul needs, you'll feel more energized and in harmony with who you truly are.

- In a reading about money, you may feel disappointed because a hoped-for payment or payoff gets delayed. Even though you're trying hard, your efforts don't bear much fruit. The time may not be right yet—don't give up.
- If the reading is about your job, you may be "hiding your light under a bushel." Perhaps you don't realize your true abilities and thus aren't

getting ahead as quickly as you could. The Star reversed can also represent disillusionment, disenchantment, or lack of inspiration.

- In a reading about love, this card can mean your expectations are unrealistic—you're searching for perfection, which can never be attained. Or, it can indicate you aren't seeing your partner or your relationship clearly.

# THE MOON: 18

*Keywords: Intuition, the unconscious, mystery, illusion, secrets*

THE MOON.

The Moon is a magical, mysterious card that symbolizes the unconscious, the realm of dreams, imagination, and psychic impressions. Some decks show the moon as full, others in its crescent phase. In the Rider-Waite-Smith deck, two canines, a dog and a wolf, howl at the moon. At the bottom of the card is a pool or pond of water from which crawls a crab (symbol of the astrological sign Cancer, ruled by the moon), crawfish, or lobster. The water suggests the moon's link with the emotions and the unconscious realm. The Moon urges you to pay more attention to your inner self, your lunar self. The light of the sun enables us to see the world around us, but the moon allows us to illuminate what springs naturally from *inside* us.

> *"Evidence of Moon worship is found in such widely varied cultures as those of the Anasazi Indians of New Mexico, the Greeks, Romans, Chinese, pre-Columbian Peruvians, Burmese, Phoenicians, and Egyptians. In the Craft, when we refer to the great god by the Hebrew names El or Elohim, we borrow terms that entered Hebrew from Arabic, where the god name 'Ilah' derives from a word that means 'moon.'"*
> —MORWYN, *SECRETS OF A WITCH'S COVEN*

## Upright

The Moon upright shows you tuning in to your lunar energies. You're becoming more aware of your feelings and inner life. The Moon also suggests psychic ability—you can sense other people's vibrations because you're connected to the information network of the invisible world. Pay attention to your dreams, feelings, instincts, and intuition. For artistic people, The Moon's appearance may indicate a time of increased imagination and creativity.

- In a reading about money, this card recommends listening to your intuition as well as your intellect in connection with a money matter. However, don't make a decision based on emotion alone. The Moon can also point to ups and downs—changing phases—in a financial situation.
- If the reading is about your job, The Moon can mean a situation has a hidden or "dark" side—this isn't necessarily bad, but you may not be aware of all the dynamics at work. Illusions or secrets may cause confusion. If you began something during the new moon, you may see things more clearly or a project may reach culmination during the full moon.
- In a reading about love, this card symbolizes a highly emotional relationship that may be tinged with illusions. Sometimes it represents a sensitive partner who nurtures you—especially creatively—or that you're working on issues of mothering and nurturing.

*"When looking for adventure in a dark and deserted landscape we should ask only for the light of the moon. Then our imaginations can create more exotic explanations for the rustling in the undergrowth or the dark (bottomless?) voids, which open up ahead of us.*

*"We comfort ourselves too much with light. Sometimes we must wander in the dark so that our other senses can find their full expression and we hear more clearly the message of the night, the wilderness and the strange creatures that inhabit the unseen spaces."*

—STEVE ROBERTS

## Reversed

The Moon card is sometimes linked with deceit and self-deception, disappointment and undoing, usually because you weren't listening to that still, small voice within. When this card appears reversed, it may advise you tie up loose ends connected to the past, especially to your mother or other women.

- In a reading about money, you may feel incapable of handling a financial matter, perhaps because you can't see what's really going on or you're too emotionally involved in the situation to be objective. This isn't the best time to make a major decision. Ups and downs are likely now; try not to let them throw you into a panic. This card can also indicate buying stuff as a way to pinch-hit for genuine emotion or happiness.
- If the reading is about your job, a secret or hidden situation may come to light. This card can also point to an emotional, uncertain, changing work environment where nothing is clear. Perhaps you've let the pressures of the outside world throw you off balance and you feel disconnected from your true self.
- In a reading about love, you've probably deluded yourself about a partner or relationship. Or, you may be attempting to cast yourself in an unreal light in order to win someone's affection. Things are not what they seem. Deceit, manipulation, or inconsistency may cause problems.

### The Triple Goddess

The moon's three aspects represent the three faces of the Great Triple Goddess. As the newborn crescent, the moon is the maiden—not chaste, but belonging to herself alone, not bound to any man. At the full moon, she is the mature woman, sexual and maternal, giver of life. At the end of her cycle, the waning moon represents the crone whose years of experience have ripened into wisdom.

# THE SUN: 19

*Keywords: Happiness, success, pleasure, self-expression, clarity, vitality*

THE SUN.

The Sun card features a blazing sun, sometimes with a face, sunbeams radiating out from it. Beneath the sun, in the Rider-Waite-Smith deck, a smiling nude child rides a white horse. Some decks show two children with their arms around each other; other decks picture a young couple holding hands. The sun rules the zodiac sign Leo, which astrologers link with children, pleasure, and creativity. The Sun card represents life itself, for the sun gives life to everything on earth. One of the most joyful cards in the tarot, it signifies vitality, confidence, achievement, attainment, and success in all endeavors.

> *"Each day comes bearing its gifts. Untie the ribbons."*
>
> —RUTH ANN SCHABACKER

## Upright

The Sun brightens any negative cards in a reading, no matter where it appears in the spread. Its influence is always beneficial. A new day is dawning and you're glad to be alive. Whatever your question, the answer is positive. For creative people, The Sun can indicate a time of increased inspiration and productivity. Whatever you undertake at this time is likely to prosper, for the sun is shining on you. This is a good time to start new projects and expand your horizons—it's your "day in the sun."

- In a reading about money, you may receive rewards for your work or talent. Investments and business ventures pay off. Opportunities abound. For creative people, this card suggests you'll benefit financially from your artistic endeavors.

- If the reading is about your job, The Sun marks a period of prosperity, enthusiasm, honors, public recognition, and attainment. You feel confident in your abilities and attract opportunities to show the world what you can do. Step into the spotlight—it's your time to shine.
- In a reading about love, The Sun represents a happy, pleasurable relationship in which you feel content and comfortable. You and your partner inspire each other and enjoy being together. If you're looking for love, this card can herald a bright and beautiful romance.

---

### The Sun King

Pagan mythology describes the apparent passage of the sun through the heavens each year as the journey of the Sun King, who drives his bright chariot across the sky. In pre-Christian Europe and Britain, the winter solstice celebrated the Sun King's birth. This beloved deity brought light into the world during the darkest time of all.

---

### Reversed

The Sun is never a negative card, but when it appears reversed it can indicate delays or that you'll have to make some adjustments you hadn't planned on. Your happiness may be more subdued, or you may feel less self-confident than if the card were upright. Perhaps you don't believe you deserve the attention, respect, or success offered to you. Or, the accolades you receive aren't as glowing as you'd expected—a four-star review instead of a five.

- In a reading about money, overconfidence may lead you to overextend yourself financially. Perhaps you feel you deserve "the best" even if your bottom line doesn't warrant it. Or, you realize you must bring your lifestyle down a notch—buy a Toyota instead of a Lexus.
- If the reading is about your job, The Sun reversed suggests you're "burning out" and need to take a break—perhaps you're overdue for a vacation. Sometimes it means you've created an inflated image, risen to a level that isn't comfortable for you, or gotten attention you don't deserve. It can also say you feel cut off from your source of inspiration or you're questioning your abilities.

*The Modern Witchcraft Book of Tarot*

- In a reading about love, the reversed Sun can represent the "drama queen" or warn that egos are interfering with your happiness. Sometimes it means getting too much of a good thing or indulging in pleasure at the expense of other things. Superficial factors—looks, money, fame—may overshadow more meaningful aspects of a relationship.

# JUDGMENT: 20

*Keywords: Awakening, self-realization, choices, assessment, rebirth*

The Judgment card often looks negative—and really, who among us likes to be judged? In the Rider-Waite-Smith deck, a winged figure (whom some interpret as the angel Gabriel) emerges from a cloud and blows a trumpet. Beneath him several nude people look up—apparently from their coffins—having heard the trumpet's blast. They outstretch their arms; their expressions reveal awe tinged with fear. This card contains overtones of Christianity's "Day of Judgment," when God judges all souls and hands out rewards or punishments. In a broader sense, however, Judgment represents a time of awakening and self-realization, when you must make adjustments to reflect who you truly are.

### Upright

Generally speaking, this is a positive card symbolizing regeneration and rebirth into wholeness after a period of confusion. I call this the "wake-up card." You're gaining self-awareness, judging your actions, choices, and life situation, determining what you want to keep and what to toss on the scrap pile. This is a time of coming clean to yourself, assessing the good, the bad, and the ugly so you can chart your course from here on with greater clarity and maturity.

*"Do not feel compelled to dance to anyone else's tune, and do not ignore the music of your own heart."*

—Barbara Moore, *The Gilded Tarot Companion*

- In a reading about money, you're facing a choice in a financial matter—the choice you make will impact not only the present but your future too. You may seek the advice of others, but only you can decide.
- If the reading is about your job, Judgment shows you're assessing your career and making a choice. Perhaps you'll decide to take a different path than the one you've been following, one that more closely aligns with your talents and objectives.
- In a reading about love, this card indicates you're facing a decision about a relationship. Judgment upright also suggests you're becoming more tolerant and less judgmental of yourself and other people.

### Reversed

Reversed, Judgment suggests you can't make a decision or won't make the changes necessary so you can move ahead. Perhaps you're confused about how to proceed. Or, you don't want to face up to harm you've done, stuff you don't like about yourself, demons you fear. You don't want to look in the mirror and see who you really are—and this can mean ignoring the good things about yourself as well as the unsavory ones. In some cases, Judgment reversed means you're too hard on yourself and others and need to become more tolerant.

- In a reading about money, you may be stuck, afraid or unwilling to make a decision about your finances—especially if you feel a change will affect your security. This card can also mean you're displeased about a legal decision or other money issue.
- If the reading is about your job, Judgment reversed suggests your current work situation no longer meets your needs, but you're reluctant to make a change because you're not clear what the future holds. This card can also mean a bad decision—your own or someone else's—has adversely affected you. Or, you may be judging yourself and others too harshly.

- In a reading about love, you may feel a partner is too critical of you—or, you may be too critical of him or her. This card can also point to a choice you made and regret or a decision you need to make but are resisting.

*"My advice to you is that it is never too late to 'fess up to what you are ashamed of having done. Hold your own judgement day and clear the slate."*

—JANE STERN, *CONFESSIONS OF A TAROT READER*

# THE WORLD: 21

*Keywords: Fulfillment, completion, achievement, mastery, wholeness*

The World represents the end of the Fool's Journey. You've trekked down an arduous path of awakening and finally reached your destination. In many decks, The World card shows a young woman, sometimes nude, holding a double-ended wand that points both upward and downward, suggesting, "As above, so below." In the Rider-Waite-Smith deck, the woman is encircled by a wreath (signifying victory) bound at the top and bottom by ribbons that call to mind the infinity symbol. She's dancing, and as Isadora Duncan believed, "One truly lives only when one dances."

Four figures in the corners signify the four elements via zodiac imagery. The World represents fulfillment—all is right with the world. You've faced your dark side and honored your beauty. I think of this as the "congratulations card." The last card of the Major Arcana, it indicates fulfillment, achievement, balance, and wholeness—the completion of the journey from innocence to enlightenment.

## Upright

Harmony reigns and you are progressing in accord with your destiny. Success is assured when The World appears upright. Everything is available to you—honors, love, happiness, abundance. Whatever you undertake now will prosper—a financial endeavor, a career move, a relationship. This card symbolizes the end of an old cycle and the beginning of a new one.

- In a reading about money, you reap the rewards you deserve. In this time of fulfillment and abundance, investments pay off, you receive what's due to you, and you realize that you have all you need.
- If the reading is about your job, you succeed because you have learned what you needed to learn, have fulfilled your potential, and are now in harmony with the universe. Everything is progressing according to divine plan. Enjoy this time of accomplishment when opportunities abound and you're free to do what pleases you.
- In a reading about love, this card represents a mature and fulfilling relationship. You've overcome your ego, fears, and insecurities; now you can enjoy a rich, happy, and harmonious partnership that's both physically and spiritually rewarding.

## Reversed

Many choices are presented to you, but you don't know which way to go. Perhaps an obstacle still stands in the way of your success. Things may get stuck, regardless of all your hard work, and you'll just have to wait until matters right themselves. Maybe the end result doesn't live up to your expectations. Sometimes you may be required to go back and do more work on something you thought you'd finished. Or, the rewards you receive are of a private, personal kind rather than worldly success.

- In a reading about money, you may need to wait a bit or work a little longer before you achieve your financial goals. Perhaps the compensation you receive is less than you'd expected. Sometimes this card shows you focusing on spiritual rather than material goals.
- If the reading is about your job, The World reversed suggests you feel restricted, frustrated, or dissatisfied with your work situation.

*The Modern Witchcraft Book of Tarot*

You thought you'd be further along by now, yet you still need to put in more effort. This card may also mean the end result isn't what you'd expected, and you feel a letdown.

- In a reading about love, a relationship may not have developed according to your plans—despite your efforts, you still see areas that need work. Don't let frustration or inertia cause you to give up—happier times may await just around the corner.

*"[T]he world is a work of art . . . neither a mechanism, nor an organism, nor even a social community—neither a school on a grand scale nor a pedagogical institution for living beings—but rather a work of divine art: at one and the same time a choreographic, musical, poetic, dramatic work of painting, sculpture and architecture."*

—ANONYMOUS, *MEDITATIONS ON THE TAROT*

---

### Shiva, God of Creation and Destruction

The World card can be linked to Shiva, the Hindu god who dances the world into being and then destroys it, only to again dance it into being, in the eternal dance of life, death, and rebirth.

---

# PART III

# Reading the Cards

# Chapter 11

# DOING TAROT READINGS

People turn to the tarot for many reasons—your motivation may not be the same as someone else's, and it may differ from reading to reading. Whether you choose to read for yourself or for others, to get advice about a pressing concern or general guidance for personal growth, remember you're dealing with a magickal device, a source of esoteric wisdom, and a tool for connecting with the Divine. Respect this exquisite oracle and don't fool around with it for mere amusement.

## THE IMPORTANCE OF ATTITUDE IN A TAROT READING

Many factors affect the accuracy and clarity of a tarot reading. Your state of mind as well as that of the person being read for (if you're reading for someone else) will profoundly influence the reading. Here, we see parallels to magick work. As a witch, you know if you don't take magick seriously or you're skeptical about your power and potential, your attitude will interfere with a spell's results. Doubt, as I've often said in connection with spellcasting, is like pouring water on a fire—it extinguishes the spell's vitality. The same holds true in a tarot reading. If you're distracted, confused, jaded, or unclear about what you seek, the answers you get will be garbled or vague.

## How Badly Do You Need to Know?

The more urgent your need to know is, the more likely you are to get a direct, definitive answer in a tarot reading. That's because you're completely focused on the matter at hand. Your subconscious, higher self, spirit guides, angels, and other helpers long to make a connection and share wisdom with you. Everything's poised to come to a head, a moment of catharsis. However, you don't want to enter a reading in a state of desperation or panic. Just relax, trust the process, and keep an open mind.

Theoretically, you already know the answer to a burning question, but you can't see beyond the blinders you're wearing. Maybe you're worrying too much or you're relying only on your logical left brain to solve the problem, searching for answers inside a cramped box with limited possibilities. The tarot can quickly cut through all that and get to the heart of the matter. The symbols on the cards provide a vehicle for opening the channels of communication between the different levels of your being—in much the same way dreams do.

---

### Negatives In, Negatives Out

If you approach a reading with a pessimistic mindset, you're more likely to get a discouraging reading than if your outlook is optimistic. If you expect a negative outcome, that's often what you'll get. On the other hand, if you keep an open mind and hope for the best, you'll have a better chance of receiving good advice.

---

## Experience, Talent, and Personal Development

Reading the tarot is like any other skill or art. Some people just naturally possess more talent than others. As a novice, you may get flashes of insight while doing a reading—even incredibly accurate insights. That's great! Go with it. However, in most cases, experience with the cards and personal/spiritual development play a bigger part in the process than innate ability. After years of working with the tarot and doing a zillion readings, you'll most likely develop a deep understanding and facility that serve you and your clients well. So even if you don't consider yourself especially psychic or gifted, don't give up—sincerity and perseverance will pay off.

Your level of spiritual development and your client's (if you're reading for someone else) can influence a reading too. If you're in touch with your own inner knowing and with the higher realms, you'll most likely glean greater meaning from the cards than someone who has a more linear, materialistic worldview. That's why witches often make excellent tarot readers—you already know how to tap your inner knowing and connect with the higher realms.

Likewise, the person you're reading for will probably gain more if he or she is open to receiving insights from sources beyond the mundane and, perhaps, has some experience with mystical studies. If you view the tarot as a teacher and vehicle for transferring insights, you'll undoubtedly be offered a great deal of valuable information.

### Record Your Readings

From the beginning of your exploration into the tarot, write down your insights, musings, and readings in a tarot journal or your witch's grimoire (book of shadows). This is especially important for novices, when you're still learning to interpret the cards and their positions in a spread. In fact, I recommend logging your readings even after you become more proficient. Keeping a record will enable you to look back and understand the information that was conveyed to you through the cards and to see how matters transpired.

# CONSULTING THE TAROT

We've already talked about the importance of approaching a tarot reading with sincerity and an open mind. What else can you do to encourage a clear, accurate, and meaningful exchange of information? Many people like to meditate beforehand to calm and center their minds. You may want to smudge the area where the reading will take place to "clear the air," just as you would before performing a magick spell or ritual. Light a candle or some incense. Invite your spirit guides to join you. Cast a circle, if you wish. Sometimes writing down your question or concern lets you clarify in your own mind what you really want to know.

## Reading the Future

If you think the future is immutable, that your fate can't be changed, I beg to differ. The future isn't fixed. Outside forces don't dictate what happens—we create our own futures. The Law of Attraction points out that we're continually creating our futures with our thoughts. Witches realize that we're co-creators with the Divine, in our individual lives and in the world around us. With our imaginations, willpower, and emotions, we affect situations in the manifest world—that's one of the main reasons we do magick spells.

A tarot reading describes the circumstances surrounding the subject of the reading—the people involved, your attitudes, social influences, natural cycles and patterns, cosmic forces, karma and/or dharma, etc. An outcome at some time in the future (if you're doing a reading that shows an outcome) is based on what's going on in the present. If the current circumstances change, so will the outcome.

## Timing in Tarot Readings

Many tarot spreads, including some presented in the next chapter, consider the past, present, and future—sometimes the near future and the distant future. "Near future" may mean a few days for one person and a few weeks for another, whereas "distant future" could indicate a few weeks to a few months, depending on the situation and the person for whom the reading is being done. As you become practiced at doing readings, you'll come to understand your own time frames.

## *What's the Shelf Life of a Reading?*

When you do a reading, for yourself or someone else, it's a good idea to remember that the indicators shown in the reading are conditional—they describe what's likely to happen if things continue as they're going along now. If you continue to act and think and feel the same way you do at the time of the reading, you'll experience the outcome that's shown. However, if factors shift along the way, if you change your ideas or behavior, the outcome could change as well.

It's probably useless to ask a question about what will happen ten years from now—too many variables can influence the outcome between the present and that date. In my opinion, a reading can look ahead only about three months, max. Outcomes do, however, occur as predicted, even over long periods. That's because most of us tend to behave and think in predictable ways and to follow prescribed, comfortable, long-standing routines.

*The Modern Witchcraft Book of Tarot*

## When's the Best Time to Do a Tarot Reading?

Some people draw a single card each morning for guidance and to see what the day might bring. You may want to contemplate that card during your daily meditation. As a witch, you understand the influence of the moon in your life, so you may decide to do a reading for yourself on each new and/or full moon. Naturally, if you're facing an important decision or pressing problem, it's an occasion to reach for your trusty tarot pack.

---

### The Illusion of "Now"

Some spiritual philosophies hold that everything is happening simultaneously—past, present, and future are illusions. That's why psychics are notoriously poor at predicting exact dates. "Now" and "future" are relative terms, and although tarot cards are good at showing what's likely to happen, they aren't quite so good at putting a time frame on it. Therefore, if you ask if something will occur within, say, a month, you may have to allow a little leeway.

---

The most holy of the witch's sabbats, Samhain is usually observed on the night of October 31. The word *samhain* comes from Irish, meaning "summer's end." Better known as Halloween or All Hallows' Eve, this is the holiday people usually associate with witches and magick. This is the witches' New Year, and it begins the Wheel of the Year. Thus, it's a time of death and rebirth.

On Samhain, we remember and honor loved ones who've passed into the afterlife or Summerland. You may attempt to contact spirits in other realms of existence on this eve or request guidance from ancestors or guardians. Because the veil that separates the seen and unseen worlds is thinnest at Samhain, it's easier to communicate with beings on the other side at this time. Therefore, it's an ideal time to pull out your tarot cards and read for yourself or others.

Your birthday is also one of the best days of the year to do magick. It's a good time to do a tarot reading too. On this special day each year, the sun shines brightly on you (even if it's raining outdoors) and spotlights your unique talents and abilities. Solar energy illuminates and enhances whatever you undertake. Your birthday also begins your personal year, a new cycle in your individual journey on earth.

In the next chapter, you'll find a tarot spread I suggest doing on your birthday, called the Horoscope Wheel. You lay out the cards in a circle, placing one card in each of the twelve houses of a horoscope wheel, and interpret them in conjunction with the astrological meanings of the houses. This gives you insight into what the coming year is likely to bring and how you can use your talents, energy, and celestial influences productively.

# THE SIGNIFICANCE OF A SIGNIFICATOR

Many tarot spreads include what's known as a significator, a card that represents you (or the person for whom the reading is being done). The significator symbolically brings you or your client into the spread and personalizes the reading.

Because the court cards (kings, queens, knights, and pages) depict people, they're popular choices for significators. Often the significator you choose relates to your sex, age, and astrological sign. It may also tie in with your profession, interests, physical characteristics, and other personal factors. For example, a Leo man over the age of thirty-five, who holds down an executive job or is active in the arts could choose the King of Wands to represent him. A sixteen-year-old Capricorn girl might choose the Page of Pentacles as her significator.

| ASTROLOGICAL SIGNIFICATORS | |
|---|---|
| King of Wands | A mature man, born under the zodiac sign Aries, Leo, or Sagittarius |
| Queen of Wands | A mature woman, born under the zodiac sign Aries, Leo, or Sagittarius |
| Knight of Wands | A young male, born under the zodiac sign Aries, Leo, or Sagittarius |
| Page of Wands | A young female, born under the zodiac sign Aries, Leo, or Sagittarius |
| King of Pentacles | A mature man, born under the zodiac sign Taurus, Virgo, or Capricorn |

## ASTROLOGICAL SIGNIFICATORS

| | |
|---|---|
| Queen of Pentacles | A mature woman, born under the zodiac sign Taurus, Virgo, or Capricorn |
| Knight of Pentacles | A young male, born under the zodiac sign Taurus, Virgo, or Capricorn |
| Page of Pentacles | A young female, born under the zodiac sign Taurus, Virgo, or Capricorn |
| King of Swords | A mature man, born under the zodiac sign Gemini, Libra, or Aquarius |
| Queen of Swords | A mature woman, born under the zodiac sign Gemini, Libra, or Aquarius |
| Knight of Swords | A young male, born under the zodiac sign Gemini, Libra, or Aquarius |
| Page of Swords | A young female, born under the zodiac sign Gemini, Libra, or Aquarius |
| King of Cups | A mature man, born under the zodiac sign Cancer, Scorpio, or Pisces |
| Queen of Cups | A mature woman, born under the zodiac sign Cancer, Scorpio, or Pisces |
| Knight of Cups | A young male, born under the zodiac sign Cancer, Scorpio, or Pisces |
| Page of Cups | A young female, born under the zodiac sign Cancer, Scorpio, or Pisces |

You aren't limited to the court cards, however. If you prefer, select a Major Arcana card to represent you. Do you feel an affinity with The High Priestess? The Emperor? Or, you might feel a connection to a card that depicts your state of mind at present—perhaps the artisan, shown by the Three of Pentacles, or a bored homemaker, symbolized by the Four of Cups.

You can choose a significator that will represent you in all readings, or you may change significators based on the circumstances of a reading. If you've recently given up your corporate job to travel around the world, for example, you may decide the Knight of Wands now describes you better than the King of Pentacles. Some people use a pendulum to dowse the proper card. Another approach is to randomly draw a significator from the pack before doing a reading—let your intuition determine who you are with respect to a particular situation.

In the next chapter, we'll start laying out the cards in what are called spreads—patterns designed to examine particular situations and impart specific information. In Part II of this book, you learned to interpret the individual meanings of the cards. Now it's time to put the cards into context. How do they relate to one another, describe the various facets of a situation, recommend action, and reveal the future?

# Chapter 12

# TWELVE TAROT SPREADS

Now it's time to start putting the individual cards into context by laying them out in patterns known as spreads. Spreads are configurations designed to convey certain types of information. Usually a spread contains three or more cards, but you can draw just one or even use the entire deck. In a spread, you don't consider only the meaning of each card; you interpret it according to the position it occupies within the overall pattern, as well as its relationship to the other cards.

---

### Synchronicity

The principle of synchronicity suggests that meaningful coincidences offer fore-knowledge of a moment in the future and that such insight is available to a person who works with the tarot. A tarot spread is a picture of that moment and everything leading up to it.

---

## READYING YOURSELF TO READ

As we discussed in the previous chapter, you may want to meditate or do some sort of ritual before you embark on a tarot reading. This helps shift your thinking from a mundane to a magickal level. I like to light a candle to symbolically shine light on the reading, and then I set a citrine (yellow quartz) crystal on top of the tarot pack to cleanse it. I keep my tarot journal handy too, so I can sketch the spread in it and record my interpretation and impressions. (Note: Remember to date your readings.)

Reading tarot is like playing a piece of music—the score is written by the original composer, but every performer interprets the music according to his or her own vision.

## Choosing Your Significator

You learned about significators in Chapters 5 and 11. Now it's time to choose yours to represent you during the reading. Most of the time I use the same significator when I read for myself—the Queen of Swords, because I'm an Aquarian woman over the age of thirty-five and my career as a writer and teacher involves communication. However, when I lay out the Celtic Cross spread, I let the deck "choose" my significator for that particular spread because I've found the card I draw represents me in the context of the specific reading—which may be different than "me" in the usual sense. Use whatever method appeals to you.

Some spreads designate a position for the significator. The Celtic Cross, for instance, hides the significator underneath card #1—you don't see it, but it's there operating in the reading. With other spreads, especially the ones that use only a few cards, you can simply lay the significator upright on the table above or to the side of the other cards.

If a spread doesn't include a place for the significator and the card chosen shows a person in profile (such as the King of Wands in the Rider-Waite-Smith deck), I like to position the card facing the spread so he or she can "watch" what's going on.

## Asking a Question

As a witch, you're probably familiar with creating affirmations. The best affirmations are stated in a simple, straightforward, unambiguous manner. The same holds true when you query the tarot for advice. Word your question clearly and concisely. Hold the question in your mind as you shuffle and lay out the cards. It may help to write the question on paper or in your tarot journal (or book of shadows).

Let's say, for example, you're considering a job offer with XYZ company. If you really want to know if you should take the job, don't ask, "Is

XYZ a good company to work for?" Even if XYZ is financially sound, highly respected, and fair to its employees, it may not be the right place for you, or the particular position you've been offered might not be your best bet.

Interestingly, the cards will show what's really important to you—even if you don't state your question that way. If you ask about your job possibilities, but your major concern is that your marriage is on the rocks and you don't know how you'll support yourself alone, that's going to come out in a reading. It just saves time and makes things easier if you clarify matters in your own mind before you begin.

*"Too often tarot cards are used to answer questions concerning lower chakra activities. For example, a question such as 'Does my boyfriend still want me?' activates first chakra survival fears, second chakra sexual concerns, and third chakra power issues. The heart is not present.*
*But the same question asked as 'What can I do to develop the best in our relationship?' can open one up to a sixth chakra creative vision."*
—SUSAN LEVITT, INTRODUCTION TO TAROT

### Shuffling the Cards

As we discussed in Chapter 5, shuffling a tarot deck not only mixes up the cards and arranges them for a reading, it also transfers your personal energy to the cards. How you shuffle will depend, in part, on the size and shape of the cards. If they're approximately the size of regular playing cards, you can riffle shuffle them. Larger cards may require you to use an overhand shuffle or other method. Some people like to place all the cards face-down on a table and mix them up randomly with their hands.

Whatever technique you decide on is okay—and when you feel you've got it right, stop. No matter how you shuffle, the cards will automatically arrange themselves as they should be—the order in which they turn up is never an accident.

### Reversed Cards

Sometimes when you lay out the cards, one or more appears upside down. "Reversed" cards are a topic of much controversy, and if you ask a dozen tarotists what they think about reversals, you may get a dozen different answers. In a recent discussion among members of an online tarot group I belong to, the Tarot Readers Development and Study Group, some members said they didn't read reversed cards, whereas other people considered it important to interpret reversals differently. In Part II, I gave you a number of possible interpretations for reversed cards in both the Minor and Major Arcana.

---

### Keep Trying

What if you don't understand the tarot's response? Try rewording your question or ask an additional question about the same issue. Perhaps the initial question was too broad or not specific enough. Keep it simple—ask only one thing at a time. But if you just don't like the answer you received, don't keep querying the oracle hoping the next reading will be better. Wait a few days before asking again—the situation or your perspective may change, thereby influencing the outcome.

---

Usually, reversed cards are said to have diminished power, sort of a tamped down version of what they'd mean if they were upright—not necessarily the opposite. The Sun upright, for example, describes happiness; reversed, it suggests contentment or a quietly joyful state, not sadness. A difficult card reversed may be less harsh or challenging than if it appeared upright.

*"In truth, reversals are ways to see though to the 'other side.' They allow us to go beyond the limits of the known."*
—MARY K. GREER, *THE COMPLETE BOOK OF TAROT REVERSALS*

Although I gave both upright and reversed interpretations for the cards, I don't think it's necessary to read reversals if you don't want to—there's certainly enough information in any tarot reading to give you the answers, insight, and guidance you need. In fact, you might be wise in the beginning, at least, to stick with reading the cards upright only. Later on, when you've become more proficient, you can explore reversals.

### Dropped Cards

Sometimes when you're shuffling or laying out the cards, one drops from the pack. This serves as a signal: Pay attention. A dropped card may point to something you haven't considered or alert you to a factor that's outside the scope of the reading but still important. You might view it as a "wild card" that skews a reading in a particular direction. It may cut right to the heart of the matter in the simplest terms, whereas the spread examines the big picture: the who, what, when, where, and why of your concern. A dropped card may make you laugh or give you chills because it's so right on; or, you may tuck it away in a corner of your mind to contemplate later. It might even show up again in your spread, in which case you can be sure someone or something is trying to get through to you!

### Shadow Cards

In Jungian psychology, "the shadow" is the dark side of your personality, the part you don't like or want to face. Consequently, this part remains hidden from your awareness. Working with the tarot can help you connect with your shadow, explore it, and heal the wounds you find within yourself.

Although people identify and work with shadow cards differently, I consider the card on the bottom of the deck—after I've shuffled and cut the pack—to represent the shadow. This card describes the shadow of the reading, a hidden dimension that underpins the situation. Of course, it also points to my own shadow and issues I'm not facing consciously.

# SINGLE CARD DRAW

Strictly speaking, this isn't a "spread," but sometimes all you need is a quick piece of advice or you want to get a sense of what the day will bring. Shuffle and cut the cards while thinking about your question. Then draw a single card from the pack. You can either pick the top card from the deck or fan out all the cards face-down and select one at random. Note your question, the card you drew, and your impressions in your tarot journal or grimoire.

# YES OR NO?

Shuffle and cut the cards while contemplating your question. Then begin laying cards face-up in a stack, one on top of the other. If you turn up an ace, stop and begin a new stack beside the first one. If you turn up thirteen cards before you come to an ace, stop. Begin a third stack beside the second one and stop when you turn over an ace or finish laying down thirteen cards.

- If you turned up two or three aces, your answer is yes. Three aces means a stronger yes than two. If the aces are reversed, you may encounter delays or problems along the way, however.
- If you only got one ace or none, your answer is no—or not at this time. One ace can leave room for hope at a later date. A reversed ace suggests a positive outcome is pretty unlikely.

Consider the suits of the aces too, as these describe the subject of the matter. Also, look at the cards on top of the stacks of thirteen. They offer additional guidance and information regarding your question.

# PAST-PRESENT-FUTURE SPREAD

This three-card spread lets you see the past influences or conditions regarding a situation, the present state of the matter, and what's likely to occur in the future. After shuffling and cutting the deck, select three cards either from the top of the pack or at random. Lay them out side by side. The card on the left represents the past, the middle card shows the present, and the card on the right indicates the future.

*Card 1:* The past
*Card 2:* The present
*Card 3:* The future

*The Modern Witchcraft Book of Tarot*

# FOUR-CARD SPREAD

This spread's strength is its simple, direct approach to dealing with practical, everyday problems. Shuffle and cut the cards, then lay four out side by side in a horizontal line, from left to right. The first card shows the situation. The card next to it represents the obstacle. The third card recommends the action you should take. The last card, on the right, indicates the outcome.

**Card 1:** *Situation*

**Card 2:** *Obstacle*

**Card 3:** *Action recommended*

**Card 4:** *Outcome*

---

### Another Four-Card Spread

You can also use a four-card spread to describe the physical, emotional, mental, and spiritual aspects of a question. The card on the left symbolizes the physical level of your question or concern, the second card corresponds to the emotional level, the third card signifies the mental level, and the card on the right represents spiritual factors.

---

# THE FIVE-POINTED STAR

Shuffle, cut, and lay out five cards at what would be the points of a star. Card 1, at the top, represents the present situation. Card 2, at the bottom left point, reveals what's hidden or what's obstructing or undermining you. Card 3, at the bottom right, shows the structures, strengths, or supports you have. Card 4, at the left-side point, indicates your fears, weaknesses, or adversaries. Card 5, at the right-side point, recommends how to best handle the situation (it can also suggest a person who can help you).

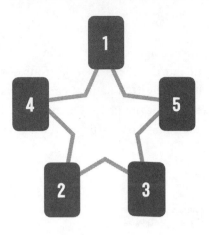

**Card 1:** *The present situation*

**Card 2:** *What's hidden or what's obstructing or undermining you*

**Card 3:** *Your structures, strengths, or supports*

**Card 4:** *Your fears, weaknesses, or adversaries*

**Card 5:** *How to best handle the situation and/or a person who can help you*

## SUPER SEVEN SPREAD

This spread shows various aspects of a situation and offers advice. After shuffling and cutting the cards, lay three cards face-up side by side; they represent the past, present, and future (just like the Past-Present-Future Spread). Next, lay two cards below this line of three; these show the influences that are hidden or that are undermining or obstructing you. Above the line of three cards, place two more cards; these recommend actions you can take and/or people who can help you.

**Card 1:** *The past*

**Card 2:** *The present*

**Card 3:** *The future*

**Cards 4 and 5:** *The influences that are hidden or that are undermining or obstructing you*

**Cards 6 and 7:** *Actions you can take and/or people who can help you*

# CELTIC CROSS

This is one of the most popular of all spreads. Arthur Edward Waite called the Celtic Cross "the most suitable for obtaining an answer to a definite question." Select a significator and place it on the table to bring you (or the person for whom the reading is being done) into the reading. Lay Card 1 on top of the significator.

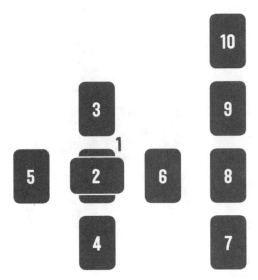

***Card 1:*** *This covers you and describes your immediate concerns.*

***Card 2:*** *This crosses you and describes obstacles facing you.*

***Card 3:*** *This crowns you and describes what's known to you objectively.*

***Card 4:*** *This lies beneath you and describes the foundation of the concern or past influences affecting the situation. It can also show what's unknown about the situation.*

***Card 5:*** *This is behind you and describes past influences now fading away.*

***Card 6:*** *This is before you and describes new circumstances coming into being in the near future.*

***Card 7:*** *This describes your current state of mind.*

***Card 8:*** *This shows the circumstances/people surrounding the situation.*

***Card 9:*** *This indicates what you hope or fear, perhaps what you hope and fear.*

***Card 10:*** *This describes the likely future outcome.*

# HARMONY SPREAD

This spread helps you find a way to resolve a dispute between two people. It symbolically depicts the two sides of an issue as two separate "pillars" and reveals three dimensions of the conflict on each side. The center card indicates how the two parties can resolve the dilemma. Notice the pattern formed is an H for harmony. You can also use this spread when two organizations need guidance in settling a conflict.

*Card 1:* This shows the root of Person A's position in the conflict and the hidden or underlying factors surrounding it.

*Card 2:* This describes the present matter from the perspective of Person A and what's known/obvious to Person A about the situation.

*Card 3:* This represents the higher dimensions of the issue and spiritual guidance available to Person A.

*Card 4:* This shows the root of Person B's position in the conflict and the hidden or underlying factors surrounding it.

*Card 5:* This describes the present matter from the perspective of Person B and what's known/obvious to Person B about the situation.

*Card 6:* This represents the higher dimensions of the issue and spiritual guidance available to Person B.

*Card 7:* The center card connects the two pillars. It suggests what can be done to bring the two parties into agreement and resolve the dispute.

# HOROSCOPE WHEEL

For this spread, you lay out twelve cards in a circle—each card corresponds to one of the twelve houses of the astrological chart. Place your significator in the center. I recommend doing this spread on your birthday, to show what's likely to happen in the coming year. You can also use it to provide information about a concern or situation, in a way similar to an event chart in astrology.

Each house in an astrological chart refers to a specific area of life; thus, you read the cards with regard to the houses in which they fall. After shuffling and cutting the cards, place one card in each house. The first house begins at the nine o'clock position, and you lay out the cards counterclockwise.

### The First House: The Self

The first house refers to your physical body and appearance, as well as your identity, sense of self, and the immediate impression you make on others.

### The Second House: Personal Resources

The second house shows what you consider valuable. This includes money, personal possessions, resources, and how you relate to what you own. It also represents your earning ability—what qualities and skills you can use to make money.

### The Third House: The Near Environment

The third house covers three areas that at first may seem unrelated, but taken together represent ordinary daily life, what astrologers call the "near environment." These are communications in your everyday life; involvement with friends, neighbors, siblings, and your community at large; and short-distance travel in your near environment.

### The Fourth House: Roots

The fourth house represents the foundation of your life—home, family, parents (especially your mother), tradition, heritage, the past, your homeland. In short, your roots.

### The Fifth House: Self-Expression

The fifth house shows your creative and self-expressive side, which may play out as artistic endeavors, romantic relationships, hobbies and amusements, or children.

### The Sixth House: Health and Service

The sixth house relates to health, health-oriented routines including nutrition and exercise, and the link between work and health. It also describes your daily work or chores, duties, job-oriented relationships, and service to others.

### The Seventh House: One-to-One Relationships

Traditionally the house of marriage and partnerships, the seventh house represents all one-to-one relationships—business as well as personal.

### The Eighth House: Transformation

The eighth is the house of the past, transformative change, death, inheritance, and other people's resources. In this case, death usually refers to the end of something old so that something new can emerge. The eighth house also shows how another person's resources (perhaps a partner's) affect you.

### The Ninth House: Higher Knowledge

The ninth house represents the higher mind, philosophy, religion/spirituality, and advanced education, as well as long-distance travel, especially to foreign lands. This house shows your search for meaning and how you go about expanding your physical, mental, and spiritual horizons.

### The Tenth House: Life Task

The tenth house represents social or professional status, career, public image, and parents (the father especially). Authority, responsibilities, honor, and reputation are tenth-house matters too.

### The Eleventh House: Friendships

The eleventh house refers to your friends and groups with which you're affiliated. Goals, hopes, and wishes are shown by this house too.

### The Twelfth House: The Hidden Realm

The twelfth house represents what's hidden, or not yet revealed, including your dreams and fantasies. It also shows your latent talents as well as fears, weaknesses, secrets, and hidden enemies. Because matters associated with this sector are often unknown to us, this house is sometimes connected with self-undoing.

# THE WORLD TREE SPREAD

This pattern is based on the Celtic pagan concept of a "World Tree," a sacred oak that connects the three realms of existence. The roots reach into the underworld, which is not the same as the Christian hell—it's the primal source from which life emerges. The trunk crosses through the earthly realm as we know it, and the branches stretch into the heavens or spirit realm. Use this spread when you want to understand the relationship between the three layers of reality or the three levels of your consciousness.

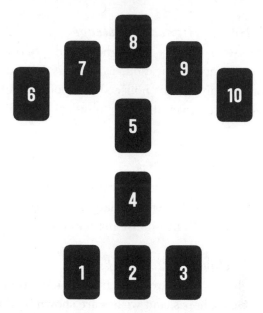

**Cards 1, 2, and 3:** *Influences in the subconscious or underworld. These three "root" cards describe the source or roots of the situation. They may exist in your subconscious, or they may be hidden spiritual forces, perhaps conditions stemming from past lifetimes.*

**Cards 4 and 5:** *The present situation. The two "trunk" cards show physical or conscious conditions and may also indicate how you're working with the forces described by the root cards.*

**Cards 6, 7, 8, 9, and 10:** *Influences in the spiritual realm or higher self. The cards that make up the branches represent spiritual forces and your higher consciousness.*

> *"A tree is one of the best examples of a motif that often appears in dreams (and elsewhere) and that can have an incredible variety of meanings. It might symbolise evolution, physical growth, or psychological maturation; death (Christ's crucifixion on the tree); it might be a phallic symbol; it might be a great deal more."*
>
> —CARL G. JUNG, *MAN AND HIS SYMBOLS*

# SPIRAL SPREAD

The spiral is an ancient symbol of life energy. This spread shows the movement from inner to outer—how core or subconscious issues evolve, emerge, and will likely manifest in the physical world.

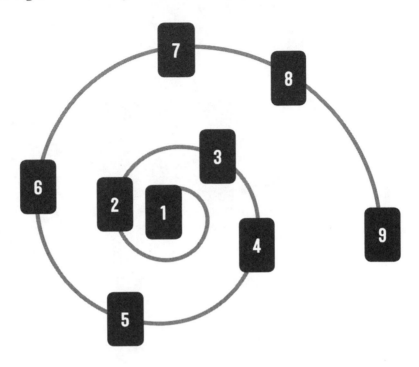

*Card 1:* This card represents the core or root of the issue.

*Cards 2 through 8:* These show the development of the matter and how it has been emerging into the querent's awareness over a period of time and, perhaps, with the influence of other people and conditions. The later cards in the spiral also offer guidance as to how the querent (the person for whom the reading is being done) may affect the outcome.

*Card 9:* This indicates the likely outcome.

# FENG SHUI SPREAD

This pattern represents the eight-sided octagon called a *bagua*, used by feng shui practitioners to examine the connections between a person's home and his or her life. The cards show the energies and influences operating in each area of your life. Interpret the cards in conjunction with the meanings of the sectors or *gua* in which they fall.

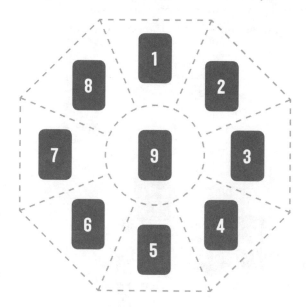

**Card 1:** *Fame, future, career*

**Card 2:** *Relationships, marriage, partnerships*

**Card 3:** *Creativity, children*

**Card 4:** *Helpful people, friends, agents/associates/colleagues, travel*

**Card 5:** *Self-image, identity*

**Card 6:** *Wisdom, knowledge, spirituality*

**Card 7:** *Family, community, neighbors*

**Card 8:** *Wealth*

**Card 9:** *Health*

You'll find lots of other spreads online and in books about the tarot. The website Psychic Revelation at www.psychic-revelation.com presents dozens of spreads for all sorts of purposes including children, pets, and health. You may even want to design your own original spreads to suit your personal needs.

# PART IV

# Using Tarot Cards *in* Magick Work

# Chapter 13

# LOVE SPELLS

The tarot provides a rich source of magickal imagery that you can tap for spells and rituals, as well as for divination. As a witch, you're familiar with using creative visualization in spellcraft. Tarot cards, with their vibrant pictures and evocative scenarios, are the perfect adjunct to magick work. They can help you focus your mind, communicate with your subconscious, and project your intentions into the outer world.

I recommend purchasing a deck specifically for spellwork and another for doing readings. That's because some of the spells you perform require you to leave the cards in place, rather than returning them to the deck afterward. In some cases, you may slip a card into a talisman or amulet pouch where it will remain for the duration of the spell. Perhaps you'd like to paste some of your favorite cards in your grimoire—I have a miniature deck that's perfect for this purpose.

> *"All love relationships mirror our relationship with ourselves. They ultimately reflect on our relationship with the world around us—how we think others see us, what we believe we are worthy of."*
> —KRIS WALDHERR, *THE LOVER'S PATH TAROT*

Because we witches tend to cast more love spells than any other kind, let's start this section with some easy and effective spells that use tarot cards to attract, enhance, or otherwise influence romantic relationships. Cards in the suit of cups describe relationships and emotions, so usually they're the ones you'll choose for love spells. However, another card may be more appropriate to a given situation or objective, such as The Lovers, Temperance, The Empress, the Four of Wands, or the Ten of Pentacles.

### Timing Love Spells for Best Results

It's usually best to perform love spells when the moon and/or sun is in Libra, the zodiac sign astrologers connect with love, marriage, and one-to-one relationships. The new moon favors beginnings; the waxing moon encourages growth; the waning moon supports letting go, decrease, and endings. Depending on your intentions, you might want to do a love spell or ritual when Taurus, Cancer, or Leo energies prevail. Venus, the planet that governs romantic partnerships, presides over the day Friday; therefore, you may choose to do love spells on Friday.

If you're already familiar with doing magick spells, you know how to cast a circle. For those of you who may be new to spellwork, witches usually cast a circle around the space where they perform magick. This psychic barrier provides protection, prevents unwanted energies from interfering, and contains your magickal power until you're ready to release it into the world. The simplest way to do this is to visualize a ball of pure white light surrounding you and the area where you're working. My books *The Modern Guide to Witchcraft*, *The Modern Witchcraft Spell Book*, and *The Modern Witchcraft Grimoire* offer a number of more elaborate circle-casting techniques.

# Drink to Your Love

*"Love is like a magic potion that once drunk leads you into the alchemy of complete transformation."*
— Manuela Dunn Mascetti, *Rumi: The Path of Love*

Japanese scientist Masaru Emoto discovered that water picks up the vibrations of pictures, words, thoughts, and emotions that come into contact with it. The water holds on to the impressions—and when you drink the imprinted water, your body absorbs the energies. This spell uses the imagery from The Lovers card in your favorite tarot deck to fill you with loving feelings.

TOOLS AND INGREDIENTS

The Lovers card

A glass of spring water

A silver (or silver-plated) spoon

A drop of melted honey or a pinch of sugar

1. Place the tarot card face-up on a windowsill where the moon will shine on it. Set the glass of spring water on top of the card and leave it overnight. The image of the card will be imprinted into the water.

2. In the morning, use a silver (or silver-plated) spoon to stir the honey or sugar into the glass to sweeten the water and, symbolically, your relationship. Stir in a clockwise direction to increase the love between you.

3. Drink the water with your partner to strengthen your love.

# Tarot Triptych Love Spell

A triptych is an altarpiece or decoration composed of three panels joined together.

TOOLS AND INGREDIENTS

3 tarot cards

Tape

Essential oil of rose, jasmine, patchouli, ylang-ylang, or musk

1.  Choose three cards from a tarot deck you don't use for readings. These cards should depict things you desire in a romantic relationship. For instance, you might select the Ten of Pentacles if financial security is important to you or the Ace of Cups if you want to attract a new partner.

2.  Lay the cards face-down, side by side, and tape them together.

3.  Dab some essential oil on each card, while you envision yourself enjoying the loving relationship you seek.

4.  Stand the triptych up on your altar or in another place where you'll see it often. If you have a mini deck or a third deck, you can affix three cards from it in your book of shadows when you record the spell. You might also want to dab a bit of essential oil on the page where you write your spell. You can adapt this spell for other intentions too—money, career success, travel. Simply select three cards that symbolize your objective.

---

## Feng Shui Magick Tip

Here's a quick and easy way to combine the imagery of the tarot with the ancient Chinese magickal practice known as feng shui. Choose a card that represents "success" or "happiness" to you (from a deck you don't use for readings). Display the card in the Relationship Gua of your home. To locate this, stand at the doorway you use most often to enter and exit your home, and face inward. The sector at the far right of your home is the Relationship Gua.

---

# Spell to Enhance a Romantic Relationship

*"Being deeply loved by someone gives you strength, while loving someone deeply gives you courage."*

—LAO TZU

Is something lacking in your relationship? Do you seek more romance, joy, passion? Choose the ingredients that symbolize what you desire. Pink candles, for example, represent love and affection, whereas red ones represent passion; rose and gardenia oils attract affection and romance; patchouli and musk have more sensual qualities.

TOOLS AND INGREDIENTS

2 candles in candleholders

Rose, ylang-ylang, jasmine, gardenia, vanilla, patchouli, or musk essential oil

A tarot card that represents you and another that represents your partner

The Nine of Cups

Matches or a lighter

1. During the waxing moon, anoint the candles with the essential oil. Put a dot of oil on your heart to open it. From your deck of tarot cards, select the King and the Queen of Cups (or two other cards to stand for you and your partner) and the Nine of Cups (the "wish card"). Place the candles on your altar, and lay the three cards face-up between the candles.

2. Light the candles and state your wish. Be specific. Imagine it coming true. After a few minutes, extinguish the candles and place them in the area where you and your beloved will be spending time together. Whenever you're together in that room, make sure these candles are burning.

# Love Talisman

Talismans attract something you desire, and this one is designed to attract a new lover. Therefore, the best time to perform this spell is on the new moon or a few days after.

### TOOLS AND INGREDIENTS

A tarot card that symbolizes your intention, such as the Ace of Cups,
the Two of Cups, the Four of Wands, The Lovers, or The Star
1 pink or red pouch, preferably made of silk or velvet
Dried rose petals
A piece of rose quartz
A piece of carnelian
A small silver or gold heart
A purple ribbon 9" long
Rose or jasmine incense in an incense burner
Matches or a lighter
Saltwater

1. Spend a few moments gazing at the tarot card you've chosen for this spell; let its imagery permeate your consciousness. If you like, you can write an affirmation that describes your intent on the card. Then put the card in the pouch.

2. Slip the rose petals (herbal symbols of love) into the pouch.

3. Wash the rose quartz (which represents love and affection) and the carnelian (which relates to passion) with mild soap and water, and pat them dry. Add them and the heart charm to the pouch.

4. Tie the pouch with the ribbon, making six knots. Six is a number of give and take, and each time you tie a knot, focus on your intention. When you've finished, say, "This is now accomplished in harmony with divine will, my own true will, and for the good of all."

5. Fit the incense into the burner and light it. Hold the pouch in the smoke for a few moments to charge it. Burning incense represents the union of fire and air (smoke), the masculine elements in the universe.

6. Dip your fingers in the saltwater, and then sprinkle the talisman to charge it with the feminine elements: water and earth.

7. Place the talisman on your altar or bedside table or in the Relationship Gua of your home.

# Spell to Restore Harmony

Has a lovers' quarrel left you and your partner at odds? Or, maybe you and your partner just aren't getting along lately. How can you mend the rift between you? By casting a magick spell, of course.

TOOLS AND INGREDIENTS

A rose quartz crystal

2 pink candles in candleholders

A tarot card that represents you and another that represents your partner

Matches or a lighter

The Temperance card

Jasmine, rose, or ylang-ylang essential oil

1.  Wash the rose quartz crystal with mild soap and water, then pat it dry.

2.  Set the two pink candles on your altar or another surface where you can leave them for three days. Position them about a foot apart. These candles represent you and your partner. (If you wish, you can inscribe your name on one of the candles and your beloved's name on the other.)

3.  Stand the cards that represent you and your partner upright facing you so that one card leans against one candleholder and the other leans against the other candleholder.

4.  Light the candles.

5.  Lay the Temperance card face-up between the candles.

6.  Anoint the rose quartz crystal with the essential oil, then set the crystal on the Temperance card.

7.  Gaze at the card as you think of your partner. Say aloud, as if speaking to your partner: "I honor the Divine within you. I forgive you and I forgive myself. I am grateful for all the good times we've known together. Let harmony reign between us. Blessed be."

8.  Continue gazing at the cards for as long as you like, allowing peaceful, harmonious, loving feelings to fill you.

9.  When you're ready, snuff out the candles.

10. Repeat the spell the next day, only this time move the two candles a little closer together. On the third day, do the spell again, moving the candles closer. This time, allow the candles to finish burning down completely. (Never leave burning candles unattended.)

# Spell to End a Relationship

Not all relationships last forever—nor are they necessarily meant to. If you've decided to end a partnership that no longer works for you, perform this spell to sever the bond peacefully. Use cards from a tarot pack you don't use for readings.

TOOLS AND INGREDIENTS

A tarot card that represents your partner

The Temperance card

The Death card

A tarot card that represents you

A piece of white cloth, preferably silk, large enough to wrap around the cards

Petals from a white carnation

A clear quartz crystal

Matches or a lighter

Pine incense in an incense burner

A shovel or trowel

1. Lay the card that represents your partner face-up on your altar (or other surface).

2. Lay the Temperance card face-up on top of the card that represents your partner.

3. Lay the Death card face-up on top of Temperance. (No, you're not casting a spell to cause your partner's death. In the tarot, Death symbolizes a transition, an ending.)

4. Lay the card that represents you facing down on top of the stack.

5. Spread out the piece of cloth and place the stack of cards in the center of it.

6. Sprinkle the carnation petals on the cards, then set the crystal on them. Wrap everything in the cloth, but don't tie the packet shut.

7. Light the incense and hold the packet in the smoke while you envision a peaceful end to the relationship.

8. Say aloud, "I release you. I thank you. I bless you. I wish you well. As we go our separate ways, may peace exist between us now and always. Blessed be." (Or, write your own parting statement, making it as simple or elaborate as you wish.)

9. Carry the packet outside and bury it in an isolated spot, away from water or trees.

## Love Spell Add-Ins

You can add other ingredients to spells to personalize or enrich them. If a symbol, object, or word holds special meaning for you, find a way to include it. Here are some suggestions:

- Crystals/gemstones: rose quartz, garnet, pearl, carnelian, opal
- Flowers: pink or red rose, jasmine, myrtle, daisy, geranium
- Essential oils/incense: jasmine, ylang-ylang, rose, patchouli, musk

*"A true soul mate is probably the most important person you'll ever meet, because they tear down your walls and smack you awake. But to live with a soul mate forever? Nah. Too painful. Soul mates, they come into your life just to reveal another layer of yourself to you, and then they leave."*
—ELIZABETH GILBERT, *EAT, PRAY, LOVE*

# Chapter 14

# PROSPERITY AND ABUNDANCE SPELLS

What do prosperity and abundance mean to you? Do you define prosperity as a dollar amount, such as a cool million, for instance? Or do you think of it as a condition or a state of being, such as living comfortably? Does abundance mean having more of everything or having enough of everything? These distinctions may seem trivial, but before you begin doing prosperity and abundance spells, you need to be clear in your own mind.

Remember, in magick work, use cards from a tarot deck you don't use for doing readings. Some of the spells you perform require you to leave the cards in place, rather than returning them to the deck afterward, such as slipping a card into a talisman or amulet pouch where it will remain for the duration of the spell.

If you're already familiar with doing magick spells, you know how to cast a circle. For those of you who may be new to spellwork, witches usually cast a circle around the space where they perform magick. This psychic barrier provides protection, prevents unwanted energies from interfering, and contains your magickal power until you're ready to release it into the world. The simplest way to do this is to visualize a ball of pure white light surrounding you and the area where you're working. My books *The Modern Guide to Witchcraft*, *The Modern Witchcraft Spell*

*Book*, and *The Modern Witchcraft Grimoire* offer a number of more elaborate circle-casting techniques.

---

### Timing Prosperity and Abundance Spells for Best Results

It's usually best to perform prosperity spells when the moon and/or sun is in Taurus, the zodiac sign astrologers connect with money and material resources. The new moon favors beginnings, the waxing moon encourages growth, the full moon brings fulfillment—plan your spells and rituals to take advantage of these lunar cycles. If your financial situation is linked to another person's resources, consider doing a spell when the moon is in Scorpio. Venus, which governs luxury, pleasure, and all sorts of material goodies, presides over Friday; therefore, you may choose to do spells to enhance abundance on Friday.

---

*"True prosperity begins with feeling good about yourself . . . It is never an amount of money; it is a state of mind. Prosperity or lack of it is an outer expression of the ideas in your head."*

—LOUISE HAY, *YOU CAN HEAL YOUR LIFE*

# Money Does Grow on Trees

The druids believed trees were sacred, and in many spiritual traditions, trees stand as central figures in the path to enlightenment. Because trees represent growth, and many trees live longer than people do, they can add beneficial energy to your spells. Before you begin this spell, select a large, healthy tree and ask it to assist you in this spellwork. (Note: It's best to perform this spell in the spring or summer, when the tree is flush with foliage. If that's not possible, choose an evergreen tree—cedar, in particular, is connected with prosperity.)

TOOLS AND INGREDIENTS

6 tarot cards that represent abundance to you

A hole-punch tool

Scissors

About 72" of green ribbon (of a biodegradable material, not plastic)

A chalice

Wine or another libation such as apple cider

1.   From a deck you don't use for readings, choose six cards that represent abundance to you.

2.   Punch a hole in each card, preferably in a spot that doesn't obliterate important symbolism.

3.   Cut six pieces of ribbon in pieces that are long enough to tie around branches or twigs of the tree you've chosen as your helper. Thread a piece of ribbon through the hole of each card.

4.   Into your chalice, pour wine or another libation. Swirl it around three times, in a clockwise direction, while you project positive thoughts into the beverage.

5.   Carry the cards and your chalice to the tree, and loosely tie the cards on small branches or twigs. Tie three knots in each ribbon, and as you tie the knots, envision abundance coming to you.

6.   When you've finished, toast the tree and thank it for its assistance. If you like, say an incantation that expresses your hopes and gratitude.

7.   Take a sip of the wine or other beverage, then pour the rest at the base of the tree as an offering.

# Goodbye Debt Spell

*"Your state of wealth externally is an extension and testament of your state of wealth internally. How clear and certain you are in thoughts of wealth is evidenced externally."*
—David Cameron Gikandi, *A Happy Pocket Full of Money*

The cauldron represents creativity and fertility; cedar is associated with wealth. Combine the two with the action of fire, and you've got a potent combination.

### TOOLS AND INGREDIENTS

A large iron cauldron (or a cooking pot if you don't have a cauldron)

Cedar wood chips, sticks, or shakes

Matches or a lighter

The Five of Pentacles

A shovel or trowel

1. Place the cauldron in a spot where it's safe to build a fire.
2. Cast a circle around the area where you'll do your spell.
3. Put the cedar inside the cauldron. Set fire to the wood, and when you have a small blaze going, drop the tarot card into the flames. (Remember to use a card from a tarot deck you don't use for readings.) The Five of Pentacles signifies debt and poverty; as the card burns, envision your debts disappearing as well.
4. Let the fire die down completely, then collect the ashes.
5. Open the circle and bury the ashes someplace far away from your home.

# Tarot Spell to Increase Your Income

The vivid colors and images on tarot cards make them a wonderful addition to any spell. Even if you don't understand all the symbols on the cards, your subconscious will register them. Candles' colors are meaningful too. Green is the color of paper money in some countries and also reminds us of healthy, growing plants. White represents clarity and protection.

TOOLS AND INGREDIENTS

A white and a green candle in candleholders

An object that represents your desire

The Ace of Pentacles

The Ten of Penacles

The Nine of Cups

The Star card

Matches or a lighter

1. Cast a circle around the area where you will perform this spell.

2. Put the candles at opposite ends of your altar. Between them, place an object that signifies your desire to increase your income. It could be a coin, a dollar bill, a piece of jewelry, or something else that suggests wealth.

3. Place the Ace of Pentacles in front of the white candle to attract new financial opportunities. In front of the green candle, put the Ten of Pentacles (sometimes called the "Wall Street card," as the ten represents a financial windfall). In the middle, between the two candles, place the Nine of Cups—the "wish card"—and The Star card, which symbolizes hope.

4. Light the candles and say:

*The money I spend*

*and the money I lend*

*comes back to me*

*in multiples of three.*

5. See money flowing to you from all directions. The more vivid you can make your visualization, the faster your wish will manifest. This spell can last as long as you want. End the spell by extinguishing the candles and giving thanks. Allow everything to remain on your altar overnight.

# Color Yourself Prosperous

As you may know, coloring books for adults have gained popularity. You can even color your own tarot cards. How cool is that? As a witch, you realize you co-create your reality in partnership with the Divine. By focusing your thoughts, feelings, and energy toward a goal, you attract the goal to you.

## TOOLS AND INGREDIENTS

A tarot coloring book or single black-and-white image of a card that represents prosperity to you (you can download these from the Internet)

Colored pencils, crayons, or colored markers

1. After selecting an image that appeals to you, set aside a place and time when you won't be disturbed. Put other cares and worries on the back burner for a while. Turn off the TV and silence your phone.

2. Establish an intention before you begin. You may want to write or state aloud an affirmation that describes your objective. If you like, write your intention directly on the coloring book page or tarot blank itself.

3. Begin coloring the image you've chosen, using whatever hues and tones appeal to you. Try to stay focused, but in a relaxed way. Don't limit yourself. If you want to color outside the lines, that's okay. The point is to enjoy yourself.

4. If you wish to create a more magickal setting in which to work, light candles, burn incense, play music, or do whatever helps you elevate your awareness.

5. Pay attention to insights, ideas, or feelings that arise while you're working. Note these in your tarot journal or grimoire.

6. Work for as long as is comfortable for you. When your attention wanes or you're no longer having fun, stop. Resume your project as soon as you can—be purposeful, but don't push yourself too hard.

7. When you've finished, display the product of your creativity where you'll see it often. Each time you see it, you'll be reminded of your objective. If you prefer, affix it in your grimoire or tarot journal. Or, put your artwork in your home's Wealth Gua (see Chapter 12 for information about feng shui).

# Quick Cash Potion

Do you need cash in a hurry? This magick potion starts working as soon as you ingest it. You can either brew this potion as a hot tea or enjoy it as a cool drink. If you like, share it with someone else whose intention is linked with your own.

TOOLS AND INGREDIENTS

A paring knife

Fresh gingerroot

Fresh mint leaves

A clear glass or cup (with no color or designs)

Spring water

Cinnamon

The Ace of Pentacles

1. Chop the ginger and mint leaves very fine—the amount you use is up to you.
2. Sprinkle them in a clear glass or cup and add the spring water. Then add a dash of cinnamon. If you wish, heat the water to make a tea but don't let it boil. (Be sure to use a glass or cup suitable for hot liquids if heating the mixture.)
3. Lay the tarot card face-up on your altar, table, or countertop and set the glass of herb water on top of it.
4. Leave it for at least five minutes to allow the image on the card to imprint the mixture with its vibrations, then drink the tea.

---

## Simple Magick

Some magick paths embrace complex rituals and practices, rich with esoteric symbolism, carefully choreographed steps, and intricate details. Kitchen and hedge witches, however, take a more relaxed approach and believe that everyday life offers us myriad opportunities to engage in magick work. Baking bread, sweeping a room, or building a fire in the hearth can be magickal acts if you view them that way. A spell needn't be complicated to be effective.

---

*The Modern Witchcraft Book of Tarot*

# Wheel of Fortune Spell

Does it seem that you never have enough money left over to buy anything extra after paying the bills? You're just scraping by. Will you ever manage to get ahead so you can treat yourself to a few luxuries? This spell helps you attract good fortune and acquire the goodies you desire.

### TOOLS AND INGREDIENTS
Pictures from magazines or printed from the Internet

Scissors

A sheet of heavy paper or posterboard

Glue, paste, or tape

The Wheel of Fortune card

1. Find pictures from magazines or print images from the Internet that depict the things you covet: a new car, a designer wardrobe, jewelry, the latest computer—whatever strikes your fancy. Cut out the pictures.

2. Cut the paper or posterboard into the shape of a circle or wheel.

3. Glue or tape the Wheel of Fortune card in the center of the paper circle. (Remember to use a card from a tarot deck you don't use for readings.)

4. Arrange the pictures you've selected around the tarot card and fasten them to the paper. As you work, imagine all these wonderful things belonging to you. See yourself driving that new car or donning those diamonds. Make your visions as real as possible.

5. Display your "wheel of fortune" vision board in a place where you will see it often. You might want to put it in what feng shui calls the Wealth Gua of your home or workplace. Each time you look at your collage, you'll reinforce your intention to draw abundance into your life.

---

### Feng Shui Magick Tip
Here's a quick and easy way to combine the imagery of the tarot with the ancient Chinese magickal practice known as feng shui. Choose a card that represents "prosperity" to you (from a deck you don't use for readings). Display the card in the Wealth Gua of your home. To locate this, stand at the doorway you use most often to enter and exit your home, and face inward. The sector at the far left is the Wealth Gua.

---

# Crystal Abundance Spell

Some quartz crystals contain bits of greenish mineral matter in them. These are known as abundance crystals. If possible, acquire one of these to use in this spell. The amplifying energy of the crystal combined with the symbolism of the color green can enhance your spell.

TOOLS AND INGREDIENTS

A quartz crystal

The Nine of Pentacles

1. Wash the crystal with mild soap and warm water to cleanse it of any ambient energies, then pat it dry.
2. Hold the crystal to your third eye while thinking about your intention; this projects the image into the crystal. The third eye, also known as the ajna chakra, is on your forehead between your eyebrows.
3. Lay the Nine of Pentacles face-up on your altar, table, or another surface. Set the crystal on the card. Make sure the crystal's point faces toward the inside of your home, to draw abundance from the universe to you. Leave the crystal in place overnight.
4. In the morning, remove the crystal and tarot card and give thanks for the bounty you are about to receive.

## Prosperity Spell Add-Ins

You can add other ingredients to spells to personalize or enrich them. If a symbol, object, or word holds special meaning for you, find a way to include it. Here are some suggestions:

- Crystals/gemstones: abundance quartz, jade, aventurine, tiger's eye
- Flowers: marigold, sunflower, yellow tulip, daffodil
- Essential oils/incense: cinnamon, clove, cedar, sandalwood, mint

# Chapter 15

# SPELLS FOR SUCCESS

Doubt, fear, and lack of self-esteem can keep you from achieving the success you desire. Ironically, your self-image probably isn't something you created yourself. It's a patchwork affair made up of bits and pieces you've collected from lots of other people and influences: family, teachers, religious leaders, your culture, and the media. Like donning clothing that's *in* style, rather than in *your* style, the self-image you wear might be uncomfortable or inappropriate. Increasing your sense of your own worthiness will help you enhance every area of your life. You'll also improve your magickal power so you can achieve better, faster results.

Remember, in magick work, use cards from a tarot deck you don't use for doing readings. Some of the spells you perform require you to leave the cards in place, rather than returning them to the deck afterward, such as slipping a card into a talisman or amulet pouch where it will remain for the duration of the spell.

If you're already familiar with doing magick spells, you know how to cast a circle. For those of you who may be new to spellwork, witches usually cast a circle around the space where they perform magick. This psychic barrier provides protection, prevents unwanted energies from interfering, and contains your magickal power until you're ready to release it into the world. The simplest way to do this is to visualize a ball of pure white light surrounding you and the area where you're working. My books *The Modern Guide to Witchcraft, The Modern Witchcraft Spell*

*Book*, and *The Modern Witchcraft Grimoire* offer a number of more elaborate circle-casting techniques.

---

## Timing Success Spells for Best Results

It's usually best to perform success spells when the moon and/or sun is in Leo, the zodiac sign astrologers connect with confidence, self-expression, and leadership. The new moon favors beginnings, the waxing moon encourages growth, the full moon brings fulfillment—plan your spells and rituals to take advantage of these lunar cycles. The sun, which rules the zodiac sign Leo, presides over Sunday; therefore, you may choose to do spells to bring success on Sunday. However, if you want to stabilize your position and establish boundaries against adversaries, consider doing a spell when the sun and/or moon is in Capricorn, or on Saturday.

---

*"There is only one success—to be able to spend your life in your own way."*

—CHRISTOPHER MORLEY, *WHERE THE BLUE BEGINS*

# Spell to Increase Self-Confidence

Because your mind is the architect of your reality, it's inevitable that your thoughts about yourself and what you deserve will generate conditions that correspond to your ideas. Therefore, the first step to success in the outer world is to elevate the way you feel about yourself inside. As Eleanor Roosevelt said, "No one can make you feel inferior without your consent." Nor can anyone else limit your personal power without your consent.

TOOLS AND INGREDIENTS

A quartz crystal

A gold or amber-colored candle

Frankincense essential oil

A candleholder

The Sun card

Matches or a lighter

1. Wash the quartz crystal with mild soap and water, then pat it dry.

2. Dress the candle with essential oil, fit it into the candleholder, and set it on your altar (or another place you prefer).

3. Lay The Sun card face-up in front of the candle and set the crystal on the card to magnify its vibration.

4. Light the candle, and then say:

*This light is presence,*

*This light is power.*

*It fills me*

*Until I am presence,*

*And I am power.*

5. Gaze at the tarot card and the crystal. Inhale the aroma of the essential oil for a few minutes, or as long as you like while you feel your personal power expanding, and then snuff out the candle's flame.

6. Leave the card on your altar or display it in a place where you'll see it often. (You can wash the crystal and use it later in another spell.) Or, if you prefer, carry The Sun with you and touch it whenever you need a confidence boost.

# Spell to Win a Decision

If an upcoming decision will affect your job, public image, or a project you're working on, use magick to tip the scales in your favor. This spell puts you in a strong position and ensures that you'll be judged fairly.

TOOLS AND INGREDIENTS

Cinnamon incense

An incense burner

Matches or a lighter

An old-fashioned set of scales or two white saucers

The Judgment card

A picture of yourself

An image that symbolizes "the other" (e.g., a person, issue, contest, etc.)

A piece of watermelon tourmaline

A gold-colored cloth

1.  Fit the incense in its burner and light it.

2.  Set the scale or the saucers on your altar or another spot where they can remain safely in place until the decision is final. If you're using a scale, lay the Judgment card face-up in front of it. If you're using two saucers, position them next to each other, about 6" apart, and lay the Judgment card face-up between them.

3.  Put the picture of yourself on the right side of the scale or in the right saucer. Put the image that symbolizes "the other" on the left side of the scale or in the left saucer.

4.  Place the piece of tourmaline (which you've washed in mild soap and water, then patted dry) on the right side of the scale or in the right saucer, along with your picture. If you're using a set of scales, the stone will actually tip it in your favor. If you're using saucers, imagine the tourmaline supporting and strengthening you, giving "weight" to your position and bringing you luck.

5.  Allow the incense to finish burning down completely while you visualize the decision being made so that you benefit. See yourself happy and successful, winning the challenge.

6.  Cover the spell components with the golden cloth. Leave the spell in place until the decision is final.

# A Light in the Darkness

*"Two things are necessary for success in life: one is a sense of purpose and the other, a touch of madness."*
—John Harricharan, www.enterprisingspirit.com

If you don't feel you're getting the attention or respect you deserve, perhaps it's because other people can't see the real you. This spell makes them sit up and take notice, as you shine your light into the darkness like a beacon.

TOOLS AND INGREDIENTS

A tarot card that represents you

7 purple candles in candleholders

Matches or a lighter

1. Begin this spell seven days before the full moon. Choose a tarot card that you resonate with or that you feel depicts you. Lay the card face-up on your altar or another spot where you can leave the spell components safely in place for a week.

2. Arrange the candles in a tight circle around the card. Light the candles, starting with the candle at the top of the card and working your way around the circle in a clockwise direction until you've lit them all.

3. Gaze at the setup for a few moments while you imagine yourself illuminated brilliantly, as if standing in a spotlight. See other people watching and admiring you.

4. When you feel ready, extinguish the candles in a counterclockwise direction.

5. The next day, repeat the ritual. This time, however, widen the circle of candles by moving each candle outward an inch or two.

6. Repeat the ritual for a total of seven days, moving the candles apart a little more each day. As the circle of candles increases in size, you expand your personal power. The light you shine into the world burns brighter and touches more people. On the night of the full moon, allow the candles to finish burning down completely to send your "light" out into the universe. (Remember not to leave burning candles unattended.)

# Self-Confidence Talisman

Whether you're interviewing for a job, giving a presentation at an important meeting, or trying to make a good impression on someone, this good luck talisman can increase your confidence and success.

TOOLS AND INGREDIENTS

A small piece of topaz or carnelian

The Emperor or Empress card

A gold-colored pouch, preferably made of silk

An almond

A pinch of sage

An acorn

A red ribbon 9" long

Matches or a lighter

Sandalwood incense in a holder

1. Wash the topaz or carnelian with mild soap and water, then pat it dry.

2. Gaze at The Emperor or The Empress for a few moments, drawing his or her power, wisdom, and confidence into yourself.

3. Slip the card into the gold-colored pouch. Add the topaz or carnelian, almond, sage, and acorn.

4. Tie the pouch with the red ribbon, making nine knots. Each time you tie a knot, repeat this incantation:

*By the magick of three times three*
*Divine power flows through me.*
*I am all I wish to be.*
*Success is mine, I now decree.*

5. Light the incense. Hold your talisman in the smoke for a few moments to charge it.

6. Carry the talisman with you to increase your self-confidence. Hold it in your hand whenever you feel a need for a confidence boost.

# Poppet Spell for Success

A "poppet" is a doll you fashion to represent a person—in this spell, it symbolizes you. In what's known as sympathetic magick, the idea is that whatever is done to the poppet happens to you.

### TOOLS AND INGREDIENTS

A poppet (a ready-made one or one you fabricate yourself from wax, straw, wood, cloth, or another material)

Objects that signify success to you, such as a crown, rich fabrics, jewelry, etc.

The Empress or Emperor card

Clippings of your hair and fingernails

Glue or tape

Matches or a lighter

Sandalwood or frankincense incense in a burner

Saltwater in a bowl or chalice

1. After you've acquired or fabricated your poppet, adorn it in whatever way represents success to you.

2. Affix the tarot card and clippings of your hair and fingernails to the poppet. If you like, you can draw "your" face on the doll or fasten a photo of yourself on it.

3. Light the incense and hold the poppet in the smoke for a few moments to charge it. Say aloud, "I charge you with fire and air."

4. Dip your fingers in the saltwater and sprinkle the poppet with it. Say aloud, "I charge you with water and earth."

5. Spend a few minutes envisioning success coming to you, filling you with satisfaction. See yourself basking in golden light; see other people honoring you; see yourself in a position you seek.

6. Put the poppet on your altar (or other place where you'll see it often). If you like, lay flowers, bay laurel leaves, gemstones, or coins at its feet as tokens of esteem.

# Hang in There Spell

We all get discouraged at times. Instead of giving up, do this spell—it helps you hang in there until the situation improves.

TOOLS AND INGREDIENTS

Oak flower essence (available in health food stores or online)

A piece of yellow paper

A pen or marker that writes red ink

A black candle in a candleholder

Matches or a lighter

A tarot card that represents you

The Strength card

The Seven of Wands

The Star card

The World card

1. Put a few drops of oak flower essence under your tongue; if you prefer, you can put the flower essence in a glass of water and drink it.

2. On the paper, draw a red pentagram at least 1 foot in diameter. Lay it face-up on your altar, a table, or another flat surface where it can remain for a time.

3. Set the candle in the center of the pentagram and light it.

4. Place the tarot card that represents you on the top point of the pentagram. Position the cards Strength and the Seven of Wands on the two side points of the pentagram. Put The Star and The World cards on the pentagram's bottom two points. Gaze at the cards and allow their symbolism to imprint your subconscious with positive imagery. Feel them stimulating the courage and confidence you need to face the challenges before you. Don't focus on your problems; just let your mind relax for a time.

5. When you feel ready or start to lose your focus, extinguish the candle. Repeat the spell as necessary, to reinforce your determination.

# Your Badge of Courage

*"Courage is its own armor."*

—Susan Oleksiw, author

Making your mark in the world, climbing the corporate ladder, finishing school, dealing with competition, even finding a way to do what you love—all take courage. This spell can help you connect with your personal power and muster the courage you need to succeed.

TOOLS AND INGREDIENTS

A tarot card that symbolizes courage to you

A pen or marker

A hole-punch tool

A piece of red ribbon about 24" long

1. On the front of the card you've chosen, write your name.

2. On the back of the card, write an affirmation to bolster your courage.

3. Punch a hole through the card near the top, being careful not to destroy important imagery, and thread the ribbon through the hole.

4. Tie the two ends of the ribbon together, making eight knots, and repeat your affirmation each time you tie a knot.

5. Slip the ribbon over your head and let the "badge" hang near your heart when you feel a need for some extra courage.

---

## Feng Shui Magick Tip

Here's a quick and easy way to combine the imagery of the tarot with the ancient Chinese magickal practice known as feng shui. Choose a card that represents "success" to you (from a deck you don't use for readings). Display the card in the Fame/Future Gua of your home. To locate this, stand at the doorway you use most often to enter and exit your home, and face inward. The sector straight in front of you, at the far end of your home, is the Fame/Future Gua.

---

## Success Spell Add-Ins

You can add other ingredients to spells to personalize or enrich them. If a symbol, object, or word holds special meaning for you, find a way to include it. Here are some suggestions:

- Crystals/gemstones: topaz, star sapphire, onyx, turquoise
- Flowers: marigold, sunflower, clover, iris
- Essential oils/incense: cedar, sandalwood, cinnamon, clove, frankincense

*"Success is measured not so much by the position that one has reached in life, but by the obstacles one has overcome while trying to succeed."*

—BOOKER T. WASHINGTON

# Chapter 16

# MISCELLANEOUS SPELLS

You can cast a spell for any reason, in any season. Witches often do spells for protection and healing. Travel spells are popular too. So are spells to mark the sabbats. You can perform an all-purpose good luck spell or design a unique one for a very special purpose. A spell may be as simple as making a wish when you blow out candles on your birthday cake or a complex ritual that takes days to enact.

Remember, in magick work, use cards from a tarot deck you don't use for doing readings. Some of the spells you perform require leaving the cards in place, rather than returning them to the deck afterward, such as slipping a card into a talisman or amulet pouch where it will remain for the duration of the spell.

If you're already familiar with doing magick spells, you know how to cast a circle. For those of you who may be new to spellwork, witches usually cast a circle around the space where they perform magick. This psychic barrier provides protection, prevents unwanted energies from interfering, and contains your magickal power until you're ready to release it into the world. The simplest way to do this is to visualize a ball of pure white light surrounding you and the area where you're working. My books *The Modern Guide to Witchcraft*, *The Modern Witchcraft Spell Book*, and *The Modern Witchcraft Grimoire* offer a number of more elaborate circle-casting techniques.

# Energy Elixir

If you're like most people, you hit a slump late in the afternoon. When you need a quick pick-me-up that's all natural and free of caffeine and sugar, drink this magick Energy Elixir to boost your vitality and clear your mind.

TOOLS AND INGREDIENTS

A clear glass jar with a lid

A small piece of rutilated quartz

Spring water

A few drops of essential oil of peppermint or spearmint

A few drops of essential oil of lemon

A few drops of essential oil of sweet orange

The Strength card

1. Wash the jar and the quartz crystal with mild soap and water, and pat dry.

2. Fill the jar with spring water. Add the essential oils, then the crystal. Cap the jar and shake it three times to charge it.

3. Lay the Strength card face-up on your altar, table, or another surface. Set the jar on the card and leave it for at least five minutes, so the water can absorb the energy of the image.

4. Remove the crystal, with your fingers, a spoon, or tongs. Sip this super-charged elixir whenever you need an energy boost.

## Timing Spells for Best Results

It's usually best to perform protection spells when the moon and/or sun is in Capricorn, the zodiac sign astrologers connect with limits, stability, banishing, and strength. Do travel spells when the moon and/or sun is in Gemini or Sagittarius. Healing spells can benefit from the energies of Virgo (the zodiac sign of health and healing), although specific conditions may respond better to other astrological energies—do some research before you begin. The new moon favors beginnings, the waxing moon encourages growth, the full moon brings fulfillment, the waning moon aids decrease and endings—plan your spells and rituals to take advantage of these lunar cycles.

# Candle Spell to Mark Midsummer

Candles represent the sun and the fire element, so burning them when the sun reaches its annual peak during the Midsummer sabbat (in the northern hemisphere) is a common way to mark the holiday.

TOOLS AND INGREDIENTS

A red, an orange, and a yellow candle

Cinnamon or sandalwood essential oil

3 candleholders

The Sun card

Matches or a lighter

1. On Midsummer's Eve, dress the candles with the essential oil and fit them into their holders. Arrange the candles in a triangle pattern with the point facing you, on your altar or another place where they can burn safely.

2. Lay the Sun card face-up in the center of the triangle. The Sun card represents fulfillment, abundance, recognition and respect, creative energy, and happiness.

3. Light the candles. As you stand in front of your altar, feel the message of the card being directed toward you and visualize yourself absorbing all that it symbolizes. Sense the candle flames illuminating you and increasing your power on every level. Imagine yourself radiating with the sun's bright light. Stand this way for as long as you like, allowing the fiery force to fill you.

4. When you feel ready, snuff out the candles and pick up the tarot card. Slip it in your pocket. Wherever you go, whatever you do the next day, you'll shine like the sun and enjoy the fullness of Midsummer.

## Invisibility

Have you ever wanted to be invisible? To accomplish this, some people say you must wear an amulet that contains seeds from forest ferns gathered on Midsummer's Eve.

# Banish the Blues

If you've been singing the blues lately, this ritual helps you change your tune. Drumming stimulates acupressure and reflexology points on your hands to produce beneficial effects. Because the beats harmonize with the beating of your own heart, the drumming makes you feel joyful and alive.

TOOLS AND INGREDIENTS

Sandalwood incense

An incense burner

Matches or a lighter

Brightly colored ribbons

A hand drum (for instance, a djembe, dumbek, or conga)

The Sun card

1. Fit the incense in its holder and light it.

2. Tie the ribbons on the drum, as many as you like, in whatever colors please you. Then attach The Sun card to the drum, with the image facing out (you may be able to simply slip it under the drum strings).

3. Begin playing the drum with both hands. Don't worry about how you sound or whether you're doing it right, just play. Feel the drum's vibrations resonating through your hands, arms, and body. Feel it breaking up the dense, depressing energy around you. Close your eyes if you like. Try a variety of beats, keeping your mind focused on your drumming. You may hear singing or sense the presence of nonphysical beings near you, for drumming attracts fun-loving spirits. If you wish, put on a CD of lively African or Caribbean music and play along with it. Continue playing as long as you like. The drum conveys the message of The Sun into the outer world, sending good vibes to all.

## Drum Magick

The oldest musical instrument, the drum also serves as a form of communication between you and the spirit world. Some people paint pictures or words of power on their drums, attach feathers or gemstones, or decorate them in various ways to convey intentions to the deities. If you like, you can fashion a talisman or amulet and tie it to the drum—each beat you play generates a resonance that helps your spell manifest.

# Tarot Travel Potion

To ensure that your trip goes smoothly and that you enjoy yourself, make this magick travel potion before you leave home.

TOOLS AND INGREDIENTS

A clear glass bottle with a lid

Spring water

The Knight of Wands

A red ribbon long enough to tie around the bottle's neck

**1.** Fill the bottle with spring water and cap the bottle, then hold it up to the moon as you say this incantation aloud:

*By the light of Lady Moon,*

*I reach my destination soon.*

*The trip shall safe and happy be,*

*For all concerned, as well as me.*

**2.** Lay the Knight of Wands face-up in a place where the moon can shine on it, and set the bottle of water on the card. Leave it there overnight.

**3.** In the morning, tie the red ribbon around the neck of the bottle, making three knots. As you tie each knot, repeat an affirmation such as "I enjoy a lovely, relaxing vacation" and visualize the end result in your mind's eye.

**4.** If you're driving, carry the bottle of magickally imprinted water with you on your trip. Sip the water periodically throughout the journey. If you're flying, drink the water before you go to the airport. As you drink, feel yourself having the perfect trip and a wonderful time away.

---

## Safety Shield

Stay safe when you travel by wearing or carrying a pentagram. This five-pointed star with a circle around it is a favorite protection amulet among witches. Hang one on a chain around your neck; tuck one in your pocket or purse; place one in your car's glove compartment—you can even draw one on your body to safeguard you while you're on the road or in the air.

---

# Amulet to Protect Your Home

As you know, witches use pentagrams to provide protection—and the suit of pentacles in the tarot is linked with this magick tool. This spell uses the Ten of Pentacles for two reasons: The number ten represents fulfillment, and this card is connected with property. In the Rider-Waite-Smith deck, the people on this card stand before their stately manor with golden pentagrams all around them.

TOOLS AND INGREDIENTS

The Ten of Pentacles

A black marker

A piece of amber

Dried basil leaves

A white drawstring pouch (preferably silk)

1. On the tarot card, write the word *safe*.

2. Wash the amber with mild soap and water, then pat dry.

3. Put the card, amber, and basil leaves in the pouch, and then close it.

4. Hang the pouch on your front door as you recite the following incantation:

*Protect this home,*

*High to low,*

*Fence to fence,*

*Door to door,*

*Light to dense,*

*Roof to floor.*

5. If you like, you can make another amulet to hang on the other door(s) to your home.

# Spell to Release Self-Limiting Patterns

*"[T]he world is a projection of our individual psyches, collected on a global screen; it is hurt or healed by every thought we think."*
—MARIANNE WILLIAMSON, *THE GIFT OF CHANGE*

What's holding you back or limiting your ability to live the happy, healthy, successful life you desire? This spell helps you cut the tie that binds you to the old pattern. Witches usually connect the color black with power, but for this spell let the black candle represent the dark or hidden side of yourself that's interfering with your fulfillment and let the white candle symbolize brighter days ahead.

TOOLS AND INGREDIENTS

A white and a black candle in candleholders

A piece of string long enough to tie the two candles together

Matches or a lighter

The Six of Swords

Scissors

1. Set the candles on your altar about 6" apart and tie them together with the string. Imagine the string is a limiting force—an attitude, habit, or something else—that keeps you from achieving what you desire.

2. Light the candles, and as you gaze at their flickering flames, feel the constricted energy of the self-limiting bond. Let your emotions come to the surface until they reach a peak and you experience a strong desire to remove the fetters.

3. Set the tarot card face-up between the two candles to signify moving away from a problem.

4. Then cut the string as you say aloud, "All beliefs, emotions, and attachments that once limited me are now removed. I am free to express myself as I choose and desire."

5. Sense the relief that accompanies this symbolic release. When you feel ready, snuff out the candles. In a fireplace, cauldron, BBQ grill, or other safe place, burn the string.

# The Magick Square

A magick square is an ancient configuration of smaller, numbered squares arranged in rows and columns in such a way that the numbers in each column and row add up to the same sum. One of the simplest magick squares, which spellcasters associate with the planet Saturn, consists of nine small squares within a larger one.

TOOLS AND INGREDIENTS

A picture of a magick square of Saturn (you can print one from the Internet or sketch one yourself)

9 tarot cards

1. Lay the magick square face-up on your altar or another flat surface.
2. Choose nine tarot cards that symbolize things you desire.
3. Lay one card in each of the nine small squares within the larger one.
4. Spend several minutes—as long as you like—gazing at the cards while you envision the items, experiences, or conditions they represent manifesting in your life.

## Feng Shui Magick Tip

Here's a quick and easy way to combine the imagery of the tarot with the ancient Chinese magickal practice known as feng shui. Look at the image of the *bagua*, pictured in Chapter 12, and mentally superimpose this design on your own home. To determine which sector or *gua* corresponds to which part of your home, stand at the door you use most often to enter and exit your home, and face inward. Choose a card that to you represents what you desire in each of these nine areas of life. (Select cards from a deck you don't use for readings.) For example, you might pick the Three of Cups for the Friendship Gua, the Nine of Pentacles for the Wealth Gua, and The Empress or Emperor for the Fame/Future Gua. Display the cards in the appropriate gua of your home.

# Yule Good Luck Charm

Would you like to give your friends and loved ones the gift of good luck in the coming year? This Yule custom lets you make a unique magickal gift for everyone on your list.

TOOLS AND INGREDIENTS

A Yule log (traditionally oak)

Matches or a lighter

A cloth drawstring pouch for each person on your gift list

Dried pink rose petals (for love)

Dried lavender buds or leaves (for peace of mind)

Dried basil (for protection)

Dried mint leaves (for prosperity)

Dried echinacea (for health)

A tarot card that represents a wish you want to come true for each of your
loved ones

1.  On the eve of the winter solstice (around December 21), build a Yule fire in a safe place and burn an oak log in it. Allow the fire to burn down completely.

2.  The next morning, after the ashes have cooled, scoop some into each pouch.

3.  Add the dried botanicals.

4.  Slip one tarot card into each pouch. For example, you might put the Nine of Pentacles in a pouch for a friend who needs a financial boost or the Two of Cups for one who seeks a happy, romantic relationship.

5.  Tie the pouches closed, bless them, and give them to your loved ones.

## Holiday Wreaths

Did you know the pretty holiday wreaths we hang on our doors during December can double as protection amulets? Witches consider pine a plant of protection and longevity. And, as you know, a circle represents safety, wholeness, and unity—that's why we cast circles around us when we do magick work. You may want to decorate your wreath with stars/pentagrams or other symbols that you associate with protection. Display an evergreen wreath on the door to your home to ward off bad vibes and ensure peace during the Yule season.

When you're comfortable with spellworking and using the tarot, you may want to design your own spells. That's great! The best spells are those that trigger your uniquely amazing creativity and imagination, touch your heart, engage your mind, and speak to you personally. If you don't feel you've got a handle on all this witchy stuff yet, you'll find lots more information, guidelines, charts, tables, etc., in my books *The Modern Guide to Witchcraft*, *The Modern Witchcraft Spell Book*, and *The Modern Witchcraft Grimoire*.

# Chapter 17

# TAKING THE NEXT STEP

You've arrived at the end of this book but not the end of your journey. Although you may have developed an understanding of the cards in your tarot pack and learned how to do readings, this just means you're ready now to move on to the next level of awareness and expertise. Like all esoteric arts and magickal paths, the tarot is infinite in scope. You will never fathom it all, no matter how many years you study this beautiful oracle or how many readings you do. New insights constantly emerge—in your own mind and in the experiences of other people, both those you read for and those whose work you read. Each insight triggers more insights. That's part of what makes the tarot so exciting!

## PRACTICE, PRACTICE, PRACTICE

Athletes and musicians know that in order to develop their talents, they must practice. The same holds true for tarot readers. Divination and magick aren't spectator sports. The more readings you do, the more comfortable you'll feel with the process and the more confident you'll become in your own ability.

### Read for Yourself

Some people say you shouldn't read for yourself, and some people feel they can't be objective when they do. I disagree. In my opinion, one of the best ways to learn the tarot is to start with yourself. Begin by picking a card each morning, to see what the day might bring. Do more in-depth readings for yourself on an as-needed basis or whenever you feel like it. Keep notes in a journal or your book of shadows so you can check back and compare your initial thoughts about the cards with what actually transpired.

### Read for Others

I also encourage you to read for your friends and relatives, if they are willing. Again, some people may argue that you can't be objective with your loved ones—and indeed, it may be difficult to share unpleasant information with them. However, you stand a better chance of seeing how matters evolve in the lives of the people close to you, which lets you judge the accuracy of your readings. When you read for strangers, you may never know whether you called it right.

---

### Consult with a Professional

If your budget allows, you may benefit from getting a professional tarot reading—or two or three. Many New Age shops either employ tarot readers or can help you contact one, and you can usually find them working at Renaissance faires and pagan festivals. You can also get free, instant tarot readings online, though I've personally never found these to be as valuable as a face-to-face consultation.

---

# EXPERIMENT WITH DIFFERENT TAROT DECKS

This book is illustrated with the Rider-Waite-Smith deck, the best-selling and most influential tarot deck in modern times. Its symbolism and storytelling imagery have inspired countless other tarot artists, and even after more than 100 years it remains a standard for both professional readers and students.

That doesn't mean it's right for you. Symbols and imagery resonate with us at deep, personal levels—what appeals to me may bore you or put you off. For instance, I find the Bohemian Gothic Tarot creepy—but that says more about me than about the artist who designed the deck. I don't like the Thoth Tarot either, although one of my most respected teachers in tarot and magick prefers it. Over the past twenty years, I've been fortunate to own and work with about 200 different decks and have finally narrowed my collection down to a dozen; the Gilded Tarot and the Aquarian Tarot remain my go-to favorites.

Experiment with a variety of tarot decks. If you feel a kinship with a deck's theme or like the artwork or sense a deck "calling to you," give it a chance. Trust your intuition. As you explore, you'll notice that some decks are designed to elicit certain insights or to teach certain things, especially those that follow particular spiritual paths—Celtic, Native American, Zen, Egyptian, etc. The book that comes with the Faery Wicca Tarot, for example, offers a lot of information about Ireland's ancient traditions in addition to the tarot. Be willing to branch out over time—what appeals to you now may not be what you'll prefer in years hence.

### DIY Tarot

You may even enjoy designing your own tarot deck, as thousands of artists have done. I've been painting my own deck for several years now, so I totally understand if you find the idea overwhelming. If you don't feel up to creating seventy-eight pieces of art, consider undertaking a joint project with friends. For example, twenty-six artists combined their talents to produce the Artist's Inner Vision Tarot. If that still seems daunting, you can purchase or download black-and-white cards, print them, and color them according to your own vision.

# EXPERIMENT WITH VARIOUS SPREADS

In Part III, I've included twelve easy-to-use spreads I like. The possibilities, however, may be infinite. Peruse other books about the tarot, as well as online sites, to see other spreads and learn how other tarotists do readings. Experiment with a variety of spreads. Most likely, you'll find yourself using some frequently and some only for special purposes.

Design your own spreads, if you wish. Consider what information you seek to gain, and then decide how to array the cards to elicit that information. Incorporate symbolism that speaks to you. For instance, a witch might relate to The Five-Pointed Star spread, an astrologer to the Horoscope Wheel (both shown in Chapter 12). Remember to sketch your original spreads in your tarot journal or book of shadows.

# EXPAND YOUR HORIZONS

Joining an online tarot group can be a great way to share ideas, gain insight from other people, learn about new tarot decks, and get answers to questions. I belong to the Tarot Readers Development and Study Group, comprised of tarot enthusiasts of various levels of expertise who engage in lively discussions about all sorts of tarot topics. I also belong to the American Tarot Association, which offers courses, a great newsletter, online readings, and lots more. If you live in a place like Salem, Massachusetts, or Glastonbury, England, you can probably find a group of tarot buddies right in your own neighborhood.

Tarot conferences can be fun and educational too—plus they're great places to network and meet like-minded folks. You may also find fellow tarotists wandering the aisles at New Age conferences and metaphysical events.

Especially when you're just beginning this journey, I recommend reading everything you can about the tarot—and there's plenty to read. Some older books may seem a bit tough to wade through, but if nothing else they'll give you a peek at the oracle's roots and what our forebears thought about the cards. Each author will offer something unique and fascinating that expands your understanding.

# MAKE YOUR OWN MAGICK

In Part IV of this book, I've included lots of spells that draw on the visual imagery of the tarot. However, these spells only touch upon what you can do when you incorporate the tarot into your magick work. Experiment with using tarot cards in your spells and rituals. If you belong to a circle, coven, or other group of magick workers, consider collaborating and sharing your spells—as well as your experiences—with the group.

Like witchcraft and magick, the tarot is a lifelong pursuit. Once it gets in your blood, it will become an integral part of your life and you'll never see things quite the same way again. The deeper you dig, the more you'll discover. Don't hesitate to veer off the main roads and amble down the narrow, winding paths where secrets and wonders abide. Everywhere you look, you'll see the tarot in action. Everyone you meet will remind you of a character you've met in the tarot. As I've said before, the tarot is a living body of knowledge and it lives all around us.

As you continue on the Fool's Journey (which never ends, by the way), keep an open mind and an open heart. Wisdom awaits on every street corner, in every flower, in every chance encounter, and every dream. You are part of the wisdom; you are part of the magick. Embrace it. Blessed be.

# INDEX

*The Modern Witchcraft Book of Tarot*

# ABOUT THE AUTHOR

Skye Alexander is the award-winning author of more than three dozen fiction and nonfiction books, including *The Modern Guide to Witchcraft*, *The Modern Witchcraft Spell Book*, *The Modern Witchcraft Grimoire*, *The Only Tarot Book You'll Ever Need*, and *Nice Spells/Naughty Spells*. Her stories have been published in anthologies internationally, and her work has been translated into more than a dozen languages. She's also a feng shui practitioner, astrologer, artist, and Reiki practitioner. The Discovery Channel featured her in the TV special *Secret Stonehenge* doing a ritual at Stonehenge. She divides her time between Texas and Massachusetts. Visit her at SkyeAlexander.com.